HIGHER

MODERN STUDIES

DEMOCRACY IN SCOTLAND AND THE UK

SECOND EDITION

Frank Cooney
Gary Hughes
& David Sheerin

Boost

HODDER
GIBSON
AN HACHETTE UK COMPANY

The Publishers would like to thank the following for permission to reproduce copyright material.

Photo credits

Chapter opener image reproduced on pages 1, 19, 35, 53, 65, 76, 101, 126, 137 © Claudio Divizia – Fotolia.

p.2 © Leon Neal – WPA Pool / Getty Images; p.5 © Wiktor Szymanowicz / Barcroft Media via Getty Images; p.7 © Sergio Azenha / Alamy Stock Photo; p.8 (top) © rnl – Fotolia; (bottom) © Eain Scott / istockphoto; p.10 © Mirrorme22 / https://commons.wikimedia.org/wiki/File:United_Kingdom_EU_referendum_2016_area_results.svg#/media/File:United_Kingdom_EU_referendum_2016_area_results_2-tone.svg / https://creativecommons.org/licenses/by-sa/3.0/deed.en; p.15 © William Edwards / AFP via Getty Images; p.20 © idp navy collection / Alamy Stock Photo; p.21 (top) © Yes Scotland Ltd; (bottom) © Better Together 2012 Limited; p.22 © epa european press photo agency b.v. / Alamy Stock Photo; p.26 © BEN STANSALL / AFP / Getty Images; p.31 © ComposedPix – Shutterstock.com; p.35 © Kay Roxby / Alamy Stock Photo; p.42 © David Cheskin / Getty Images; p.54 (left) © C Squared Studios / Photodisc / Getty Images / European Objects OS44; (right) © Tyler Olson – SimpleFoto / Fotolia.com; p.61 © Mark Severn / Alamy Stock Photo; p.69 (left) © Hannah McKay-WPA POOL / Getty Images; (right) © Xinhua / Alamy Stock Photo; p.71 © Jeremy Corbyn / Twitter; p.72 (top left) © Snapchat; (bottom right) © PA Images / Alamy Stock Photo; p.75 © Twitter, Inc.; p.76 © Roger Gaisford / Alamy Stock Photo; p.78 © Colin Fisher / Alamy Stock Photo; p.79 © Scottish Government (Attribution 2.0 Generic (CC BY 2.0)); p.89 © Ken Jack / Alamy Stock Photo; p.96 © Ken Jack / Alamy Stock Photo; p.103 (top) © LESLEY MARTIN / AFP / Getty Images; (bottom) © Sarah Owen; p.108 © PA Images / Alamy Stock Photo; p.111 © PA Wire / PA Archive / Press Association Images; p.112 © PA / PA Archive / Press Association Images; p.119 © WILL OLIVER / EPA-EFE / Shutterstock; p.120 © Leon Neal – WPA Pool / Getty Images; p.127 © David Cliff / SOPA Images / LightRocket via Getty Images; p.129 © Craig Redmond / Alamy Stock Photo; p. 131 © Daniel Reinhardt / dpa / Alamy Live News / dpa picture alliance / Alamy Stock Photo; p.133 © Steven Scott Taylor / Alamy Stock Photo; p.134 © Michael Kemp / Alamy Stock Photo; p.136 © Chris J Ratcliffe / Getty Images; p.137 © David Sheerin; p.140 © David Sheerin.

Acknowledgements – see page 142

Orders: please contact Hachette UK Distribution, Hely Hutchinson Centre, Milton Road, Didcot, Oxfordshire, OX11 7HH. Telephone: +44 (0)1235 827827. Email education@hachette.co.uk Lines are open from 9 a.m. to 5 p.m., Monday to Friday. You can also order through our website: www.hoddereducation.co.uk. If you have queries or questions that aren't about an order, you can contact us at hoddergibson@hodder.co.uk

© Frank Cooney, Gary Hughes, David Sheerin 2021

First published in 2021 by
Hodder Gibson, an imprint of Hodder Education
An Hachette UK Company
211 St Vincent Street
Glasgow, G2 5QY

Impression number   5   4   3   2   1

Year   2025 2024 2023 2022 2021

Cover photo © Lukasz Stefanski/Shutterstock.com
Illustrations by Integra Software Services Pvt. Ltd., Pondicherry, India
Typeset in Minion Pro 12/15 by Integra Software Services Pvt. Ltd., Pondicherry, India
Printed in Italy

A catalogue record for this title is available from the British Library.

ISBN: 978 1 5104 5778 2

Contents

1 The UK constitutional arrangements

The structure of the government

The UK is a parliamentary democracy with a constitutional monarch as head of state. The present monarch, the Queen, has no political power, and the royal prerogatives are exercised by the prime minister and government ministers, who in turn are responsible to an elected House of Commons (see box 'The constitutional monarchy'). While Americans might refer to the monarch as the Queen of England, she is queen to the people of England, Northern Ireland, Scotland and Wales and to the people of the 15 realms of the Commonwealth.

In the UK all powers are invested in the UK Parliament and this is referred to as parliamentary sovereignty. However, membership of the European Union (EU) and acceptance of the European Convention on Human Rights (ECHR) have diminished parliamentary sovereignty. The Conservative government is considering abolishing the Human Rights Act and replacing it with a British Bill of Rights (see pages 4–5). The Conservative government held a referendum on the UK remaining within the EU in June 2016 (see pages 8–10). In its 2017 manifesto, the Conservatives stated that the government would reassess the rights of UK citizens once the UK had left the EU.

The constitutional monarchy

Prerogative functions

The British monarch retains some long-standing common law powers known as royal prerogatives. The present monarch, Queen Elizabeth, became queen in 1952 and is the longest serving monarch. The royal family plays a very visible part in British politics even though these powers are exercised by the prime minister. The Queen and Prince Charles are routinely informed about policy decision making and have access to confidential papers. Prince Charles, for example, sends numerous letters to government ministers outlining his views.

Opening parliament

The parliamentary year runs from the date when the monarch 'summons' (opens) parliament until the date when it is 'prorogued' (closed). The monarch reads out the government's major policy proposals, which is currently referred to as the 'Queen's speech'.

Dissolution of parliament

The maximum term of any parliament is five years, at the end of which the monarch declares that the parliament is dissolved. Prior to the parliament of 2010–15, the prime minister could use this power to dissolve parliament at any point during the five years. Since then, the UK has had fixed-term parliaments. However, Prime Minster Boris Johnson has stated his intention to restore this prerogative power.

⇨

Appointing the prime minister and first minister

The monarch still 'appoints' all ministers of the Crown including the executive heads of government. By convention the leader of the largest party is usually invited to form a government. This government is referred to as 'Her/His Majesty's government'.

The royal assent

A bill that has passed through the required legislative process in the Houses of Parliament and devolved assemblies must receive the royal assent from the monarch before it becomes law.

Symbolic functions

Head of state

It is the monarch rather than the prime minister who is head of state. In the USA the president is head of state.

Head of the Commonwealth

The monarch is the head of the 'Family of Nations' and usually opens Commonwealth conferences.

Figure 1.1 **The Queen opening parliament**

The British constitution

A constitution is a set of rules that lays down the powers and duties of the institutions of government and establishes the rights and liberties of citizens.

Unlike all other major states the UK does not have a written constitution. Critics argue that this is a major flaw in our democratic structure. We may have conventions and statute law, but a government with a majority is often described as an 'elected dictatorship' with little effective scrutiny from parliament. In contrast, the US Constitution limits the power of the Executive through the separation of powers between the different branches of government. An American president envies the powers of a UK prime minister.

No UK party has won a general election with more than 50 per cent of the vote since 1935, yet the winning party usually wins a majority of seats in the House of Commons. This enables the government to use this majority to govern as it wishes with limited checks to its powers. This is described as an elected dictatorship as the Legislature cannot check the actions of the Executive (the opposite of the American system). As an example of this, in 2003 Prime Minister Tony Blair went to war against Iraq without consulting parliament.

The UK's constitutional arrangements are uncodified, which means that the rules that govern our country can be amended relatively easily through parliamentary statutes (laws such as the 2011 Fixed-term Parliament Act – see page 3). Further, many of the parliamentary procedures and constitutional principles are based not on laws but on 'convention' (see page 3). Important conventions such as collective cabinet responsibility have become established principles and practice of cabinet government.

Parliamentary democracy

The Executive part of government is drawn from the Legislature and is, in turn, accountable to it.

Royal prerogative

Powers of the monarch that are exercised in the Crown's name by the prime minister and government ministers.

Devolved

Powers that have been transferred from central government to local or regional administration.

Referendum

The electorate, not their representatives, vote to accept or reject a proposal.

2011 Fixed-term Parliament Act

This Act is an example of how a previously unwritten part of the constitution can be replaced by a codified statute. Prior to this Act the convention was that the prime minister, using the royal prerogative power of dissolution, had the right to decide when a general election would be held during the parliament's five-year term.

Under the above Act a general election was held on the first Thursday in May 2015. The subsequent election was to be held in May 2020; however, parliament agreed at the request of Prime Minister Theresa May to hold a general election in May 2017. It also agreed to Prime Minister Boris Johnson's request to hold another election in December 2019.

Examples of constitutional conventions

- The House of Lords does not oppose legislation contained within the government's manifesto (the Salisbury Convention). However, the Liberal Democrat peers rejected this government mandate in 2005. They argued that the Labour government had been elected by only 35 per cent of the vote and the Liberal Democrat peers voted against the introduction of identity cards, a policy within the Labour election manifesto.
- The prime minister is the leader of the largest party – or coalition of parties – in the House of Commons.
- Money bills are the responsibility of the House of Commons.
- The monarch grants royal assent to all parliamentary legislation.

- Individual ministerial responsibility requires a minister to resign following significant departmental failure.

Constitutional conventions that are now codified

The Sewel Convention established that Westminster would not legislate on matters affecting devolved administrations without their consent. In 2005 this convention was codified and enshrined within parliament's Standing Orders as Legislative Consent Motions. However, the Conservative government ignored the Scottish Parliament's refusal to ratify the EU Withdrawal Agreement, thus highlighting the sovereignty of the UK Parliament and the limited powers of the Scottish Parliament.

The convention that the prime minister chooses the date of an election (within a five-year period) was ended by the 2011 Fixed-term Parliament Act (see box '2011 Fixed-term Parliament Act').

Should the UK have a written (codified) constitution?

No

- Our uncodified constitution provides flexibility. It can adapt to changing circumstances and to political pressure. An excellent example is the creation of the Scottish Parliament and the granting of further powers to the Scottish government. The UK constitution has adapted to EU membership and reform of the House of Lords, which further highlights its flexibility.
- As implied, it is easy to change and it works. There are no cumbersome arrangements to change the constitution, unlike in the USA. It can be changed by a simple Act of Parliament. The present system has been continually tested and proved worthy.
- It usually ensures strong and accountable government. In the UK model, there is usually no conflict between the Executive and the Legislature. Contrast this with the USA and the failure of President Obama to pass key legislation through a hostile Republican-controlled Congress.
- Parliamentary sovereignty is at the centre of our constitution and this enables a party with a majority in the House of Commons to deliver its election manifesto. Both Margaret Thatcher and Tony Blair introduced significant political, social and economic change to Britain. Contrast this with President Obama's failure to achieve new gun control laws.

Yes

- A written constitution provides clarity. It is usually contained in one single document and is clear and accessible to all citizens. It is easy to understand and everyone can refer to it when necessary. Its lack of ambiguity should reduce the possibility of political disputes.
- It provides limited government and in theory should encourage consensus government.
- A written constitution within a democracy prevents the Executive becoming too powerful. The US Constitution enshrines the separation of powers between Executive, Legislature and Judiciary to ensure that the president does not become a dictator. In contrast, the UK Executive has been called an elected dictatorship, whereby a government elected with only a minority of the popular vote can make profound changes to the UK constitution. In the 2019 general election, the Conservatives with less than 45 per cent of the electoral vote achieved an overall majority of 80 Members of Parliament (MPs). This enabled the government to take the UK out of the EU.
- It protects human rights. A written constitution guarantees the rights of its citizens through a document referred to as the Bill of Rights. This document is enshrined within the constitution. This can prevent the state abusing its powers under the cloak of national security.

Abolition of the Human Rights Act

The Conservatives' manifesto in 2015 stated that the party would scrap the Human Rights Act, which had been passed in 1998 by the Labour government. In practice, the Act has two main effects. Firstly, it incorporates the rights of the European Convention on Human Rights (ECHR) into domestic British law. What this means is that if someone has a complaint under human rights law they do not have to go to European courts but can get justice from British courts. Secondly, it requires all public bodies – not just the central government, but institutions like the police, National Health Service (NHS) and local councils – to abide by these human rights.

⇨

It is important to note that the ECHR has nothing to do with the EU and predates it by decades. Its institutions and courts are completely separate. Ratification of the convention is a condition of being a member of the EU. (Every European country except Belarus – Europe's last military dictatorship – is a member of the ECHR.)

Successive Conservative governments have talked about replacing the Human Rights Act with what they call a 'British Bill of Rights'. They argue this new bill will 'break the formal link between British Courts and the European Court of Human Rights'. In practice, this would likely mean that people who wanted to bring human rights cases under the ECHR would have to go to a court in Strasbourg, France, to be heard.

The Scottish government has strongly opposed any move to abolish the Human Rights Act. In the face of strong opposition the Conservative government of Prime Minister May set up a working group to reconsider the issue. However, in 2019, Boris Johnson stated that he would review the Human Rights Act following the implementation of the new Brexit trade deal. In the first round of post-Brexit talks in March 2020, UK officials confirmed to the EU that the government did not wish for ECHR membership to be included in a future trade agreement.

The UK Judiciary

One hallmark of a democracy is the existence of an independent judiciary and over the last few decades judicial independence in the UK has been strengthened.

Actions to strengthen the Judiciary

- The Constitutional Reform Act 2005 set up the independent Supreme Court as the highest court in the UK. To further ensure judicial independence, the Lord Chancellor is no longer the head of the Judiciary. This ensures that government ministers are barred from trying to influence judicial decisions through direct access to judges.
- Judges are being increasingly appointed by the Judicial Appointments Commission rather than by the government. However, the prime minister can exercise their power to veto appointments.
- Judges of the High Court and above can only be dismissed by both Houses of Parliament.

Figure 1.2 **British Supreme Court judges**

Conflict between Judiciary and Executive

With the threat from international terrorism there can be tension between protecting the rights of citizens and maintaining state security. Successive governments have been unhappy that judges have opposed Executive action, citing the Human Rights Act. On numerous occasions the then home secretary, Theresa May, criticised the legal decisions of judges. For example, there have been cases of criminals managing to avoid government deportation orders to their home country by citing Human Rights Act Article 8 'Right to a family life'.

Parliament prorogation and the Supreme Court

The Brexit crisis has involved the Judiciary in the political decision making of the government. In September 2019, the Supreme Court was required to rule on the legality of Prime Minister Johnson's decision to prorogue (suspend) parliament. Although the English lower court had supported the government, the Supreme Court rejected the government's claim that the request was simply to provide more time for ministerial preparation ahead of the Queen's Speech in mid-October. It ruled that it was to prevent parliamentary discussion and scrutiny of the government's Brexit negotiations and planning and, as such, the prime minister's advice to the Queen to prorogue parliament was unlawful. The Scottish court had also ruled that the suspension was illegal.

Show your understanding

1 Outline the prerogative powers of the monarchy.
2 Give three examples of constitutional conventions.
3 Outline the arguments for and against a written constitution.
4 In what ways has the judicial independence of the Judiciary been strengthened in recent years?
5 Why is there opposition to the Conservatives' pledge to abolish the Human Rights Act?
6 Why, in September 2019, did the Supreme Court declare the actions of Prime Minister Johnson as being unlawful?

Research activity

Should the UK have a written constitution? Working in pairs, investigate this issue and present your findings to the class.

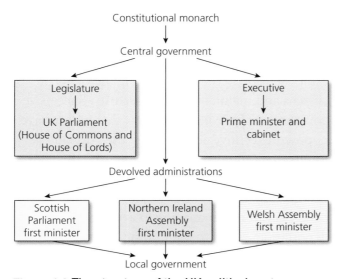

Figure 1.3 **The structure of the UK political system**

The role and powers of the devolved bodies

We now have devolved parliaments (assemblies) in Northern Ireland, Scotland and Wales that can pass laws linked to their devolved powers. All these laws must receive the royal assent from the Queen as advised by the prime minister. However, the powers devolved to the three parliaments can be returned to the UK Parliament and the devolved parliaments dissolved. (The Scottish National Party (SNP) proposed that the Scotland Act 2016 should recognise the permanence of the Scottish Parliament – it was blocked by Westminster Conservative MPs.)

The UK central government has responsibility for national affairs such as immigration, defence, foreign policy and the environment. In the UK, the prime minister leads the government with the support of the cabinet and ministers. Departments and their agencies are responsible for putting government policy into practice.

In Northern Ireland, Scotland and Wales, some government policies and public services are different from those in England. The UK central government has given certain powers to devolved governments, so that they can make decisions for their own areas. The arrangements are different for each, reflecting their history and administrative structures.

Welsh Assembly

The National Assembly for Wales is the representative body, with law-making powers on devolved matters. It debates and approves legislation. The role of the Assembly is to scrutinise and monitor the Welsh Assembly government. It has 60 elected members and meets in the Senedd.

Northern Ireland Assembly

The Northern Ireland Assembly was established as part of the Belfast Agreement (also known as the Good Friday Agreement) in 1998. Devolution to Northern Ireland was suspended in October 2002 and restored on 8 May 2007. However, the Assembly was once again suspended in January 2017 when the coalition between the Democratic Unionist Party (DUP) and Sinn Féin broke down as the parties were in dispute. Power-sharing was finally restored in January 2020.

Scottish Parliament

The Scottish Parliament held its first election in 1999 and a coalition government of Labour and Liberal Democrats was set up (see Table 2.1, page 19). The Scottish Parliament debates topical issues and passes laws on devolved matters affecting Scotland. It also scrutinises the work and policies of the Scottish government. It is made up of 129 elected Members of the Scottish Parliament (MSPs), and meets at Holyrood in Edinburgh. Its devolved powers such as education are listed in Table 1.1. However, more powers continue to be devolved to Scotland. As part of the 2012

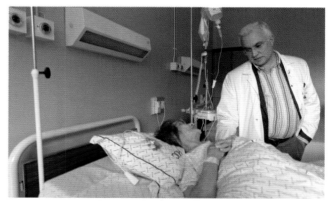

Figure 1.4 **The Scottish government is responsible for health**

Act, MSPs at Holyrood are now responsible for laws on airguns and drink-driving limits. During the 2014 Scottish Referendum campaign, the three main UK parties promised far greater powers to be granted to the Scottish Parliament. This was to persuade Scottish voters to remain within the UK. This promise of further powers – called devo-max – became the blueprint for the Scotland Act of 2016 (see pages 27–28).

Table 1.1 **Reserved and devolved powers of the Scottish Parliament (2020)**

Reserved issues include:	Scottish devolved powers include:
<ul><li>Constitutional matters</li><li>UK foreign policy</li><li>UK defence and national security</li><li>Fiscal, economic and monetary system</li><li>Immigration and nationality</li><li>Energy: electricity, coal, gas and nuclear energy</li><li>Common markets</li><li>Trade and industry, including competition and customer protection</li><li>Some aspects of transport, including railways, transport safety and regulation</li><li>Employment legislation</li><li>Shared social security</li><li>Gambling and the National Lottery</li><li>Data protection</li><li>Human fertilisation, embryology and genetics</li><li>Equal opportunities</li></ul>	<ul><li>Education and training</li><li>Health (control of abortion was added in 2015 as part of the Scotland Act)</li><li>Local government</li><li>Social work</li><li>Housing</li><li>Planning</li><li>Tourism, economic development and financial assistance to industry</li><li>Some aspects of transport, including the Scottish road network, bus policy and ports and harbours</li><li>Law and home affairs, criminal and civil law, the prosecution system and the courts</li><li>Shared social security and control of income tax rates</li><li>Police and fire services</li><li>The environment</li><li>Natural and built heritage</li><li>Agriculture, forestry and fishing</li><li>Sport and the arts</li></ul>

Figure 1.5 **Westminster (top) and Holyrood**

Show your understanding

1 Describe the structure of the UK political system. (You should refer to the UK political system and devolved administrations.)
2 Outline the main devolved powers of the Scottish government in the period 1999–2020.

The EU Referendum, 23 June 2016

The UK has been a member of the EU since 1973 and over the years greater economic, social and political co-operation and integration has had a significant impact on decision making in the UK. Critics argue that the UK Parliament is no longer sovereign and that EU edicts must be implemented. A common criticism of the EU is that, with the free movement of all

European citizens, overly high numbers of workers have come from Eastern Europe, taking British jobs and the generous welfare benefits that the UK offers. Supporters argue that British citizens have had the right to attend European universities and work anywhere in the 27 countries that make up the EU. Workers from other EU states contribute to our economy, and Scotland with an ageing population has benefited from an influx of young workers and their families.

The referendum campaigns for both the 'Remain' and 'Leave' parties were criticised for their negativity. Even the SNP agreed with Brexit supporters that the UK government had waged a 'Project Fear' campaign on behalf of 'Remain', with George Osborne warning that a 'Leave' vote would lead to an emergency austerity budget.

The turnout on the day of 72 per cent was 6 per cent higher than the level in the May 2015 general election. Supporters of the 'Remain' campaign went to sleep on Thursday 23 June confident that the UK would remain in Europe – the financial market had indicated thus. The view of the City was that the British public had seen through the half-truths of the 'Leave' campaign. These included the London bus with the distortion that we paid £350 million every week to the EU; the claim that Turkey was about to join the EU (implying that many of its 75 million citizens would seek to immigrate to Britain); and a widely criticised UK Independence Party (UKIP) campaign poster, which many felt had racist overtones.

Yet the 'Remain' supporters – the majority of them young, educated Scots, Irish and Londoners, according to the polls – woke up on Friday morning to the new reality that the UK would be leaving the EU. UKIP leader Nigel Farage triumphantly declared 23 June as 'independence day for England'. The 'Leave' message that Britain should 'take back control' of its own affairs from the EU had been a very effective slogan.

The reason for Vote Leave's victory was simple – it appeared that the key issue for many voters was not free trade but immigration. Voting turnout in the areas of England and Wales that had suffered deindustrialisation and the impact of the savage austerity cuts was high. The view of many who felt forgotten was that voting in elections was a waste of time, but they would vote 'Leave' in the EU Referendum as a protest. The political and social fault line between England and Scotland had widened.

Commentators have suggested that David Cameron must surely regret his gamble to resolve the internal conflict in the Conservative Party by calling the EU Referendum. To his critics, he is the prime minister who needlessly ended our EU membership and his action could possibly lead to the break-up of the UK.

Table 1.2 **June 2016 EU Referendum results across the UK (%)**

Nation/Region	'Remain'	'Leave'
UK	48.1	51.9
England	46.6	53.4
Northern Ireland	55.8	44.2
Scotland	62.0	38.0
Wales	47.5	52.5
Selected regions of England		
West Midlands	40.7	59.3
Yorkshire/Humber	42.3	57.7
South East	48.2	51.8
London	59.9	40.1

Key results and immediate consequences

- All of Scotland's 32 councils voted to remain in the EU.
- Moray, with the fishing industry at its heart, had the slimmest 'Remain' majority – just 122 votes.

- Edinburgh had the strongest city vote for 'Remain' at 74.4 per cent.
- Only 56.6 per cent of Glasgow's electorate voted – the UK's lowest turnout.
- Gibraltar had the biggest vote for 'Remain' at 95.6 per cent, and the strongest turnout of 83.5 per cent.
- Only 27 per cent of young voters voted to leave, compared to 60 per cent of elderly voters.
- David Cameron announced he would resign as prime minister and that the Conservative Party would not only choose their new leader but the next prime minister.
- Nicola Sturgeon would explore all options to keep Scotland in the EU, including the strong possibility of holding a second referendum on Scottish independence. She stated: 'Scotland faces the prospect of being taken out of the EU against our will. I regard that as democratically unacceptable.'
- Sinn Féin called for a border poll on Irish unity as a consequence of the Brexit win. Inhabitants of Northern Ireland and the Republic of Ireland have the right to claim a passport from the Republic and thus remain EU citizens.
- Labour leader Jeremy Corbyn was heavily criticised for his lack of leadership during the referendum campaign and was blamed for Labour supporters voting 'Leave'. He was criticised for not showing enthusiasm for the EU.
- Theresa May won the Conservative leadership election and became the new prime minister.

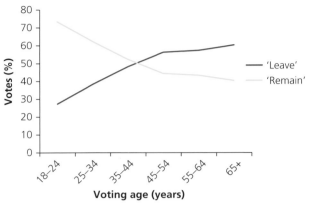

Figure 1.6 **Votes cast in the June 2016 EU Referendum by voting age**
Source: Lord Ashcroft Poll

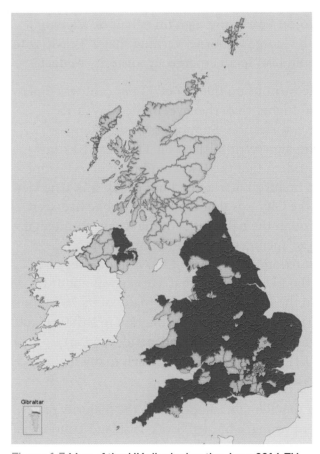

Figure 1.7 **Map of the UK displaying the June 2016 EU Referendum results (blue = 'Leave'; yellow = 'Remain')**
Source: Wikimedia Commons

Table 1.3 **Factors for and against the UK remaining in the EU**

The UK should remain in the EU	The UK should leave the EU
Political benefits	*Political factors and sovereignty*
The UK may have given up some national powers as a member of the EU. However, we have gained a voice within the global power that is the EU. We have greater international standing reinforced by our permanent seat in the UN Security Council. We also can provide serious military support to resolve conflict situations. Our international standing would be weakened if we left the EU. The threat from international terrorism, economic recession and the refugee crisis requires a united EU response.	The UK would regain its national sovereignty and the UK Parliament and courts would not need to enforce EU directives. The Westminster Parliament would once again have parliamentary sovereignty. We would have greater control over who can enter our country.
Economic benefits	*Economic alternative to EU membership*
The EU is the world's largest single market with a total GDP greater than that of the USA. The single market of over 500 million people with no custom duties or tariffs provides great opportunities for British businesses. The UK government estimates that 3.5 million jobs are linked to the UK's trade with other member states. It is true that Norway and Switzerland, who are not members of the EU, have strong economic ties. However, Norway has had to adopt 6,000 EU legislative Acts – without any say in the creation of these Acts.	The UK is a member of the World Trade Organisation (WTO), which has trade agreements with over 50 countries. As such the UK can leave the EU and still continue to trade with partners such as Switzerland. Also the UK pays more into the EU than it receives – an estimated net contribution of £10 billion (in 2018–19, the net contribution was £8.9 billion).
Individual benefits	*Eurozone economies are in crisis*
Membership gives all UK citizens the right to study, work, live and have their pension paid into any EU nation. Students can apply to and attend universities abroad. Numerous EU directives ensure better consumer protection, including compensation for airport delays. We now have cleaner beaches, safer food and better animal protection.	Numerous countries have faced serious financial difficulties, which have led some to label the eurozone a financial disaster. The rush to economic unity through the adoption of the euro has brought misery and unemployment to millions of EU citizens.
Democratic deficit?	*Democratic deficit?*
The decision-making process within the EU is said to lack accountability and as such there is a democratic deficit within the EU. However, the influence of the European Parliament has increased in recent years and it should not be forgotten that decisions made by the unelected Council of Ministers are decisions made by ministers from elected governments including Britain.	Decisions that impact on British citizens are made by faceless bureaucrats in Brussels and some claim this is destroying British values and traditions. British taxpayers are subsidising French and other European farmers. The EU has been described as a 'gravy-train "for those who work in it"' – the total budget for EU administration is estimated at £34 billion per annum. The Common Fisheries Policy (CFP) has been a disaster for the Scottish fishing industry as the UK gave traditional UK fishing waters to the EU.

Negotiations between the UK and the EU

29 March 2017 Prime Minister May submits Article 50, the formal process to leave, needed to begin negotiations.

2017–19 Negotiations take place on the EU Withdrawal Agreement with the original deadline of 29 March 2019. The agreement reached between the UK government and the EU is rejected by parliament on several occasions. The main objection is over the Irish backstop agreement, which was opposed by many Conservative MPs and their Northern Ireland allies, the DUP. The proposed agreement would prevent a trade border being set up in the island of Ireland. Northern Ireland would remain in the EU Customs Union. The DUP argues that this would threaten the unity of the UK.

July 2019 Boris Johnson becomes the new prime minister and successfully negotiates a new withdrawal agreement, which is opposed by the DUP.

December 2019 The Conservative prime minister Boris Johnson wins a landslide general election with a clear mandate and a strong parliamentary majority to deliver Brexit.

31 January 2020 The Withdrawal Bill comes into effect and the UK leaves the EU. All final negotiations and agreements must be complete by 31 December 2020, which could lead to a no-deal Brexit.

February 2020 The Conservative government announces a new points system that will end unskilled European workers entering the UK.

March–August 2020 The spread of COVID-19 around Europe effectively places on hold meaningful negotiations between the EU and UK on a new trade agreement. Michael Barnier of the EU urges the UK to extend the transition date beyond 31 December 2020. He accuses the UK government of 'running down the clock' with the strong possibility of a no-deal Brexit.

September 2020 As part of the UK Internal Market (UIM) Bill, the UK government confirms that it includes changes to the Withdrawal Act that break international law. This move is condemned by the international community and by former UK prime ministers.

October 2020 The Scottish Parliament vote to reject approval of the UIM Bill on the grounds that it breaks international law and threatens devolution. The bill is designed to harmonise trade and to reallocate powers and financial aid at present implemented by the EU. The new powers will reside with the UK government even when they cover devolved areas such as agriculture. The Scottish government calls this a 'power-grab' (see also page 29).

24 December 2020 The EU and the UK sign a trade agreement a week before the UK officially leaves the EU. The deal means that tariffs will not be imposed on UK or EU goods. However, this does not cover services such as finance. A compromise agreement also covers fishing, which disappoints the fishing industry (see pages 15–16). Below are the key points:

- British citizens no longer have the right to live or work in the 27 EU countries and in return the UK has complete control of its borders. As they are no longer EU citizens, British people will be treated as 'third country nationals'. Those who wish to stay in the EU for a longer period to study or spend time in their second home will face significant restrictions. The Erasmus scheme, whereby British students could study abroad, has been ended by the UK government. It will be replaced by a UK global scheme.

- The problem of Northern Ireland still remains. The solution was to leave Northern Ireland in the EU's single market for goods and as such EU custom rules will be enforced at Northern Irish ports. Goods travelling from Great Britain will need new paperwork; for example, animal products will need export health certificates. Northern Irish students can still participate in the Erasmus scheme. Despite Boris Johnson stating that Northern Ireland has 'the best of all worlds', the Unionist community is unhappy that it is not fully part of the UK and faces trade restrictions with the rest of the UK. The Unionists want the border in the Irish Sea scrapped. However, this would mean a hard customs border between the north and south of Ireland, which would upset the Irish Republicans.

While the trade agreement means no tariffs, significant barriers for UK business still remain. Leaving the single market and custom checks means an extra layer of paperwork and veterinary checks (if required) that will increase costs and delay the exports of UK goods.

January–April 2021 The resurgence of COVID-19 with a return to a national shutdown distracted the public from the economic impact of Brexit. Indeed, the major success of the UK's vaccination programme compared to the slow roll-out in the EU was declared by the UK government as a triumph for Brexit. The 27 countries of the EU had given responsibility to the European Commission for buying and sharing out COVID-19 vaccines. According to figures released by Our World in Data in late April 2021, 70 vaccine doses had been administered per 100 people in the UK, compared to just 30 doses per 100 people in France, Germany, Italy and Spain. However, Malta, an EU country, had a higher figure than the UK, at 73 doses per 100 people.

Any problems created for UK industry in terms of trade to the EU were dismissed as 'teething troubles' by the UK government. The paperwork and checks now required mean that seafood exporters can no longer get seafood to the EU within 24 hours. In response, the UK government announced a £23 million compensation package for seafood exporters.

The possible impact of the UK leaving the EU

In June 2016, the UK public voted narrowly to leave the EU (England and Wales voted to leave, and Scotland and Northern Ireland to remain). But what had they voted for: was it for a hard Brexit with no free trade with the EU, or was it for a soft Brexit with the UK, for example, staying in the **single market**? What was certain was the country was divided, with Remainers arguing that

any agreement should be endorsed by the British public through a second referendum.

Single market – the European single market includes all EU countries. Other countries may join as long as they accept the following: free movement of goods, people, services and capital.

Customs union – all countries within the customs union apply a common tariff (tax) for goods imported from countries outside the bloc.

Key aspects of a soft Brexit

- It would keep the UK closely linked with the EU as the UK would stay in the single market and customs union. (Non-EU countries can be members of the single market (for example, Norway) and customs union (for example, Turkey).)
- The UK would be bound by some of the rules and tariffs (taxes) of the EU but have no say in how these rules are made. It would be almost impossible for Britain to do any trade deals with third (other) countries such as the USA.
- While the Scottish government wishes to stay in the EU, it proposed a soft Brexit in order to minimise the negative economic consequences of a hard Brexit.
- A soft Brexit would minimise the impact on trade and business, especially the car industry and London's financial market – the City of London earns around £205 billion a year from European demand in financial services, such as banking and investments. This would reduce the financial cost of Brexit, as trade would not be interrupted.
- The Northern Ireland peace agreement would not be under threat as the present trade agreements would continue between Northern Ireland and the rest of Ireland.

Key aspects of a hard Brexit

- The UK would leave both the single market and customs unions and, once the divorce bill had been paid, the UK would be free from all EU regulations and financial costs and would regain its sovereignty.
- There would be no free movement of EU nationals and the UK would control its borders.
- The UK would be able to negotiate favourable new trade arrangements with the EU during the transition period. The UK would also be able to negotiate new trade agreements with third countries.
- There might be short-term damage to the economy but once the UK negotiated its new deals with other countries the economy would prosper.
- The UK could negotiate a deal that protects the Irish peace agreement and meets the economic needs of Northern Ireland.

In his election campaign, Boris Johnson had urged the UK public to vote for the Conservatives, thus giving them a mandate to 'Get Brexit Done'. He promised that final transition negotiations would be straightforward and swift, and, in his words, a final agreement was 'oven-ready'. As such, the UK would formally leave the EU on 31 January 2020 with a withdrawal deal. This would be followed by a transition period, with the UK leaving the EU on 31 December 2020. The prime minister stated that there would be no further delays and that an agreement had to be agreed by 31 December 2020. EU negotiators questioned this optimism and all were concerned that the UK could leave with 'no deal'.

In the transition period both sides should agree to a new trade deal and the details of the future UK relationship with the EU – including law enforcement, access to fishing waters, security and data sharing. If a deal is not agreed then checks and tariffs on UK goods entering the EU will need to be enforced.

Summary of the Withdrawal Agreement Bill

- There is to be no extension to the transition period beyond 2020, even if no free trade deal agreement has been reached.
- During the transition period, the UK will continue to make its full financial contribution to the EU and follow EU laws.
- The European Communities Act, which took the UK into the EU, will end at the end of 2020.
- New custom arrangements will create a customs and regulatory border between Northern Ireland and Great Britain. Some goods entering Northern Ireland from Great Britain will pay EU import tax which would be refunded if goods are not moved to the Republic of Ireland.
- During the transition period, the UK can hold formal meetings with non-EU countries such as the USA to negotiate trade deals.
- The original agreement of Prime Minster May to safeguard workers' rights has been removed, as well as the scrutiny role of parliament.

The Common Fisheries Policy

Figure 1.8 **60 per cent of the UK's total catch is landed in Scottish ports**

The EU had announced that a fishing deal was a precondition to any wider agreement and the deal had to be completed by November 2020. Fishing is a very emotional issue for people who feel the industry was sacrificed when the UK joined the EU: this meant Britain became subject to quotas set in Brussels and British waters were opened up to European fleets. Boris Johnson had pledged that any agreement had to ensure that 'British fishing grounds are first and foremost for British boats.' The reclamation of the fishing industry had become emblematic of setting Britain free from the shackles of EU restrictions.

Under the Common Fisheries Policy (CFP), all member states have equal access to EU waters with the exception of the 12 nautical miles around the UK coast. At the end of 2020 the UK became an independent coastal state, operating under the UN Convention on the Law of the Sea and with control of 200 nautical miles of its shores.

The EU wanted to negotiate a new deal that would still allow EU countries to fish in these waters. There had been threats by EU politicians that the UK's access to the EU's lucrative financial market depended on a fishing access agreement. This was no idle threat as the value of financial services to the UK is £132 billion. (The fishing sector is worth £784 million to the UK economy.) Further, Jean-Yves Le Drian, the French minister of Europe and foreign affairs, stated that, if European boats were barred from UK waters, France would press for British trawlers to be prevented from selling their catches to EU countries. This was a particularly significant issue for Scotland – despite having only around 8 per cent of the UK population, over 60 per cent of the UK's total catch is landed in Scottish ports.

In December 2020 a compromise agreement was reached that displeased the UK fishing industry. The main points are in the box on the next page.

- The UK fishing industry will only 'take back' 25% of the EU catch in UK waters until 30 June 2026. After that, annual negotiations will be held on sharing out the catch between the UK and the EU. An arbitration body will be set up to resolve fishing disputes.

- The UK will have the right to completely exclude EU boats from 2026. However, the EU can retaliate with taxes on exports of British fish to the UK or by denying UK boats access to EU waters.

The impact on immigration

A hard Brexit enables the UK to control its borders and in February 2020 the government announced its new immigration policy. Europeans will no longer benefit from free movement as the government places emphasis on attracting skilled workers, with no entry allowed for workers deemed to be unskilled (see box 'UK points-based immigration system'). The home secretary, Priti Patel, encouraged employers to invest in technology for automation and stated that there were 8 million 'economically inactive' people aged 16–64 available to replace the European workers who would no longer be able come to the UK to work in low-skilled employment. The government argued that the availability of low-paid European workers kept wages low and using UK citizens would lead to higher wages, making the jobs more attractive. However, it has been pointed out that one of the sectors that employs high number of immigrant workers, social care, is underpaid because it relies on skills that are undervalued by society. The government is indirectly the largest employer of care workers and in fact it can be said that government cuts to funding actually hold down wages – average earnings in the care sector are between £17,000 and £20,000.

Nicola Sturgeon who had been pushing for immigration to be devolved to the Scottish Parliament was dismayed by the proposed new policy, as were the tourist, farming, fishing and care industries.

Reaction in Scotland

- Nicola Sturgeon, SNP leader: 'It is impossible to overstate how devastating this UK government policy will be for Scotland's economy. Our demographics mean we need to keep attracting people here, this makes it so much harder.'
- Jackson Carlaw, Scottish Conservative leader: 'The plan would open a door to more skilled staff for our universities and high-tech sectors.'
- NFU (National Farmers Union) Scotland stated that increasing the Seasonal Agricultural Workers Scheme still leaves the number of seasonal workers available 'woefully short' of the 70,000 required for farming in the UK.
- Stephen Leckie, chairman of Scottish Tourism Alliance: 'The approach from [Priti Patel] on automation … is staggering. …Care sectors, farming, hospitality and retail just don't work that way … show me a robot which can make a smoked salmon sandwich … Hospitality and tourism is all about people, it can't be automated.'
- Professor Rebecca Kay, University of Glasgow: 'The areas of Scotland which most need people are most likely to be the areas which don't have jobs which meet the salary threshold … jobs in sectors which are being defined as low skilled, generally having depressed salary rates, and in areas which desperately need people to come, not just to work but to settle and have families.'

UK points-based immigration system

- From January 2021, EU and non-EU citizens will be treated equally, with preference given to highly skilled workers via a points system, with 70 points required for eligibility (see Table 1.4). (Highly qualified is now classified as having at least an A level or Scottish Higher qualification.)
- The salary threshold for skilled workers will be reduced to £26,500 from £30,000, and for designated shortage occupations, such as nursing, it will be lowered to £20,480.
- There will be no immigration route for low-skilled workers, which will impact on recruitment in hospitality, agriculture and the care services. According to the government's policy document: 'We will not introduce a general low-skilled or temporary work route. We need to shift the focus of our economy away from a reliance on cheap labour from Europe and instead concentrate on investment in technology and automation. Employers will need to adjust.'
- The Seasonal Agricultural Workers Scheme will be expanded from 2,500 to 10,000.

Table 1.4 **UK points-based immigration system**

Characteristics	Tradeable	Points
Offer of job by approved sponsor	No	20
Job at appropriate skill level	No	20
Speaks English at required level	No	10
Salary of £20,480 (minimum)–£23,039	Yes	0
Salary of £23,040–£25,599	Yes	10
Salary of £25,600 or above	Yes	20
Job in a shortage occupation (as designated by the MAC [Migration Advisory Committee])	Yes	20
Education qualification: PhD in subject relevant to the job	Yes	10
Education qualification: PhD in a STEM [science, technology, engineering and mathematics] subject relevant to the job	Yes	20

Source: www.gov.uk

Show your understanding

1 Outline the outcome of the June 2016 EU Referendum.
2 Outline the arguments for and against the UK remaining in the EU.
3 Explain the difference between a hard and a soft Brexit.
4 a) Why is UK fishing such an emotive issue?
   b) Why might a compromise on the fishing policy between the UK and the EU be the best outcome?
5 a) Describe the new immigration policy introduced in 2021.
   b) What are the advantages of the new immigration policy?
   c) Why has it been criticised by the Scottish government and by the hospitality and farming communities?

Show your understanding

12-mark question

Analyse the potential impact of leaving the EU.

You should refer to issues affecting Scotland or the UK or both in your answer.

Added Value idea

Organise a class debate on the motion:
Leaving the EU will make the UK 'great again'.

2 Scotland and its constitutional future

Background

In 1979 the people of Scotland voted in a referendum on the setting up of a Scottish Assembly. Although there was a narrow victory for the 'Yes' vote, it failed to achieve the artificial threshold of 40 per cent of the electorate voting 'Yes', and so no Scottish Assembly was set up.

From 1979 to 1997 the Conservative Party was in power in the UK and introduced policies that were unpopular in Scotland. It also rejected any form of devolution for Scotland. However, in 1997 the new Labour government led by Tony Blair held a referendum to ask the Scottish people if they wanted a Scottish Parliament. In September 1997 the outcome of the referendum was a resounding 'Yes', with more than 74 per cent voting for the setting up of a Scottish Parliament.

The Scottish Parliament

In 1999 the Scottish Parliament came into being, and usually every four/five years Scotland elects 129 MSPs and a Scottish government to be responsible for the devolved powers given by the UK Parliament. Since 2007 the SNP has formed the Scottish government with a platform of greater powers for the Scottish Parliament (see Table 2.1).

All three unionist parties – Labour, Conservative and Liberal Democrats – are against independence for Scotland. However, all three parties support greater powers being granted to the Scottish Parliament (albeit with slightly different versions). This is referred to as devo-max.

Table 2.1 **Elections and governments of Scotland 1999–2021**

Election	Government formed
1999	Labour and Liberal Democrats coalition
2003	Labour and Liberal Democrats
2007	SNP minority
2011	SNP majority
2016	SNP minority
2021	SNP minority

The Calman Commission 2007–09

This Commission was set up in December 2007 to recommend any changes to the Scotland Act of 1998 that would enhance the role of the Scottish Parliament. It published its final report in June 2009.

The Scotland Act 2012

As a result of the Calman Report, and consensus among all of the UK parties, the UK coalition government granted further devolved powers to Scotland. The Scotland Act 2012 granted the Scottish Parliament greater taxation and borrowing powers and limited legislative powers over drugs, driving and guns. Scotland used these new powers to reduce the drink-driving limit from 80 mg to 50 mg per 100 ml of blood. This Act came into force in December 2014.

To the surprise and dismay of all the unionist parties, the SNP won the 2011 election by a landslide (the Additional Member System (AMS) of voting had been designed to prevent the SNP winning a majority).

With a clear mandate from the Scottish people, the SNP began negotiations with the Westminster government to hold another referendum on Scottish independence. Finally in October 2012 both David Cameron and Alex Salmond signed the Edinburgh Agreement, which promised a referendum to be held before the end of 2014, and a reduction in the voting age to 16.

Figure 2.1 **The UK's Trident nuclear deterrent is based at Faslane on the Clyde**

The Scottish Referendum, 18 September 2014

On 18 September 2014, the people of Scotland voted in a referendum on the constitutional future of Scotland. In a campaign that lasted for 30 months the people of Scotland were energised by the debate and the voters engaged in the discussion around the referendum question.

The question asked, to which voters were required to vote either 'Yes' or 'No', was: *Should Scotland be an independent country?*

The road to the referendum

May 2011

The SNP won a majority in the Holyrood elections and the Scottish Parliament passed a historic and symbolic vote to hold a referendum on independence.

October 2012: The Edinburgh Agreement

After months of tense negotiations, Scottish First Minister Alex Salmond and UK Prime Minister David Cameron signed an agreement to hold a one-question referendum by the end of 2014. The SNP persuaded the UK government to change the electoral law to allow 16- and 17-year-olds to vote.

November 2013: White Paper on Independence

This 670-page White Paper sets out the case that an independent Scotland would have a strong economy and would be able to create a positive partnership with the remaining UK nations.

Independence White Paper

Below are some of its key statements:

- Scotland needs to tackle inequality both in wealth and health and can only achieve this by having complete control over pensions and welfare and the benefits system. The introduction of the bedroom tax and Universal Credit would be reversed.
- The NHS would remain in public hands and the privatisation of the NHS would be ended.
- Independence would make life better for Scots, and Scotland would take its place among member states of the EU and UN.
- Independence would address Scotland's 'democratic deficit' – 'for 34 out of 68 years since the Second World War, the nation has been governed by governments in Westminster that have no majority here'.
- It would be a modern, European democracy, founded on a written constitution with the Queen as head of state.
- It would create a new Scottish Broadcasting Service (SBS) and the Royal Mail would be brought back into public ownership.

The respective campaigns

Yes Scotland

YesScotland

In May 2012 Alex Salmond launched the campaign for independence and in terms of political parties Yes Scotland was supported by the SNP, the Scottish Greens and the Scottish Socialists. The general consensus was that the 'Yes' campaign had been enthusiastic, positive and people-centred. Yes Scotland, the umbrella group that orchestrated volunteers in 300 local groups, can take part of the credit for the highest ever level of voter registration in electoral history: 97 per cent and an 85 per cent turnout. Yes Scotland provided local campaigns with funds, merchandising and information. Their campaign was described as a 'festival of democracy'. New groups also emerged such as the left-wing Radical Independence Campaign, which sent activists into Labour's stronghold housing estates. In one week in August 2014 this group door-stepped 18,000 voters in 90 working-class communities.

Better Together

bettertogether

In terms of political parties Better Together was supported by Labour, the Conservatives and the Liberal Democrats, with Alistair Darling (Labour) the leading figure. Its campaign to persuade the Scottish people to reject independence was launched in June 2012 by the Scottish leaders of these three unionist parties. Director of Better Together Blair McDougall, a Labour Party national campaigner, concentrated on the uncertainties of independence and ran a negative campaign referred to as 'Project Fear' by the 'Yes' campaign. The Better Together campaign focused particularly around the future of Scotland's currency. Then Chancellor of the Exchequer George Osborne stated that 'if Scotland walks away from the UK, it walks away from the UK pound'. Such a move would damage the Scottish economy and banking industry and the statement from the banks that they would have to move their headquarters to England frightened many Scots. There would be no amicable divorce. As political commentator Iain Macwhirter wrote, 'There was very little attempt by Better Together to offer a positive vision of a new progressive partnership between Scotland and England. It was a grudging "No" vote brought by threats and negativity.' For many Scots, especially the young, there was an impression that the rest of the UK (rUK) would put the Scottish economy at risk rather than let Scotland create a mutually beneficial new economic partnership with rUK.

Show your understanding

1 Compare the types of government formed between 1999 and 2016.
2 Outline the devolved powers given to the Scottish Parliament by the Scotland Act 2012.
3 Outline the arguments for and against an independent Scotland.
4 Compare the campaign tactics of Yes Scotland and Better Together.

Result of the 2014 Scottish Independence Referendum

The Scottish people voted to remain in the Union by a margin of 55 per cent to 45 per cent. A 'Yes' voter summed it up by saying: 'fear won over faith and greed over glory' (see voting analysis below). Opinion polls over the previous two decades had consistently stated that only 30 per cent of Scots wanted independence, yet a 'rogue' poll shortly before the referendum indicated that the 'Yes' vote had gained such momentum that it would achieve a majority result (in the weeks running up to elections the 'Yes' vote had increased to about 40 per cent). This created panic in Westminster, with the leaders of the three major parties rushing north to support Gordon Brown's high-profile campaign to persuade the Scots to reject independence. The three leaders issued the signed 'Vow' that the Scottish Parliament would receive more powers if independence was rejected (see *Daily Record* front page of 16 September 2014 – page 26).

Figure 2.2 Two 'Yes' supporters draped in Scottish colours after the result

Turnout and patterns of voting

In all, 85 per cent of Scottish people turned out to vote in the referendum. In some regions, such as East Dunbartonshire and Stirling, turnout was over 90 per cent, the highest turnout ever recorded in a UK election or referendum (the lowest turnout was in Glasgow at 75 per cent). Four councils returned a majority 'Yes' vote – Dundee, Glasgow, North Lanarkshire and West

Dunbartonshire – while the remaining 28 voted 'No'. This resulted in claims from many that the poorest in society had voted for change while in more affluent areas people had been more likely to vote to remain part of the UK. It was also clear that a majority of the over-60s and female voters voted 'No' (see Table 2.6).

However, it was widely acknowledged that even a 'No' vote was not a vote for the status quo and that the people of Scotland demanded change. Following the result Alex Salmond announced that he would stand down as party leader and as first minister. Nicola Sturgeon was elected party leader and became the first female first minister.

Table 2.2 **Results of the referendum: Should Scotland be an independent country?**

	Votes	%
Yes	1,617,989	44.7
No	2,001,926	55.3

Table 2.3 **Turnout: The three highest and three lowest councils (%)**

East Dunbartonshire	91.0	Glasgow	75.0
Stirling	90.1	Dundee	78.8
East Renfrewshire	90.4	Aberdeen	81.7

Table 2.4 **The four highest 'Yes' votes (local authorities)**

	Yes (votes)	Yes (%)
Dundee	53,620	57.3
West Dunbartonshire	33,720	54.0
Glasgow	194,779	53.4
North Lanarkshire	115,783	51.1

Table 2.5 **The four highest 'No' votes (local authorities)**

	No (votes)	No (%)
Orkney	10,004	67.2
Borders	55,553	66.5
Dumfries & Galloway	70,039	65.6
Shetland	9,951	63.6

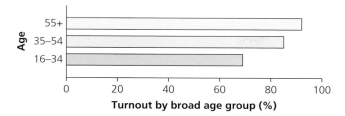

Figure 2.3 **Turnout by broad age group**

Table 2.6 **Gender, age and social class (%)**

	Men	Women	60+	Under 60	ABC1	C2DE
Yes	49	43	31	50.5	42	49
No	51	57	69	49.5	58	51

Source: Based on Lord Ashcroft poll and YouGov polls

YouGov is a British internet-based market research and opinion polls company that is respected worldwide.

Lord Ashcroft is a Conservative peer who carries out detailed opinion polls. He is not a member of the British Polling Council, which sets standards for the industry.

Voting pattern

The initial two voting pattern polls taken by Lord Ashcroft and YouGov immediately after the referendum suggested that there was a clear split between older and young voters, between male and female voters, and that low earners backed independence (see Table 2.6).

Table 2.7 **Voting patterns by religious affiliation (%)**

	Yes	No
Protestant	39.9	60.1
Catholic	57.7	42.3
Church of England	19.4	80.6
Other	52.5	47.5
None	52.1	47.9

Source: Scottish Referendum Survey 2015

However, a survey report published in September 2015 suggested that this was not the full picture. The Scottish Referendum Survey, based on a survey of 5,000 Scots and conducted a few days after the election, questioned some of these assumptions. The survey suggested that the 'No' vote could be explained by an alliance of Scotland's younger voters, its average earners, Protestants and women.

Voters earning more than £30,000 were evenly split, while those earning less than £20,000 were 53 per cent for independence. The surprising figure was that those earning between £20,000 and £30,000 were only 44 per cent for independence. While it was true that older voters favoured Scotland remaining part of the UK, the youngest voters, aged between 16 and 24, also delivered a 'No' to independence majority. Those aged 25 to 29 were the age group most likely to vote 'Yes', with 62 per cent for independence.

The survey also confirmed that those born in other parts of the UK but living in Scotland were overwhelmingly against independence with a resounding 70 per cent voting 'No'. Educational background had no significant impact. However, religious affiliation had a strong impact: 60 per cent of Protestants voted 'No', while 58 per cent of Catholics voted 'Yes'. The conservative unionist Protestant organisation, the Orange Order, had campaigned for a 'No' vote and this partly explains the religious divergence.

Table 2.8 **Voting patterns by annual income (%)**

	Yes	No
£0–£19,999	53.2	46.8
£20,000–£29,999	45.5	54.5
£30,000–£39,999	49.8	50.2
Over £45,000	49.5	50.5

Source: Scottish Referendum Survey 2015

Role of the media

The media played an important part in the propaganda war between the two camps during this time. The 'Yes' camp was very effective in the use of social media including Twitter and had its own online magazine – *Bella Caledonia*.

New social media can also be an avenue of misinformation, as well as abuse and malicious propaganda. Some 'cybernats' – nationalist supporters – were accused of making abusive remarks towards prominent unionists such as J.K. Rowling, which damaged the nationalist cause. While the media gave massive coverage to attacks on Rowling and the entrepreneur Michelle Mone, cyber attacks on pro-independence women such as Elaine C. Smith failed to achieve as much coverage in the media.

Newspapers

Newspaper coverage was mostly hostile to independence. The *Sunday Herald* became the only Scottish newspaper to openly support it. On 3 May 2014, in a striking front page designed by the Scottish writer and artist Alasdair Gray, the newspaper declared its support. The massive imbalance in support between the 'Yes' and 'No' campaigns was reflected in the referendum coverage in the press, with negative stories dominating overall by about three to one. Some were rather absurd: for example, *The Mirror* claimed that Edinburgh's giant pandas might

have to be sent back to China if independence was achieved. The *Daily Express* front page headline of 8 June 2014 was: 'UK split to set back cure for cancer'. And again on 3 September: 'Yes vote risks EU veto and Wonga style interest rates'. Scotland-based newspapers such as the *Daily Record* were also guilty of scare-mongering stories: its headline on 12 September was that independence 'could trigger a new Great (world) Depression'.

Television

Research conducted after the referendum highlighted the importance of television coverage during this time, with a significant majority of people (71 per cent) stating that television and radio were important sources of information (see Figure 2.4). Central to the impact of television were the two television debates between the leaders of the campaigns and the BBC Big Debate, which gave an opportunity for the 16–17 age group to express their opinions.

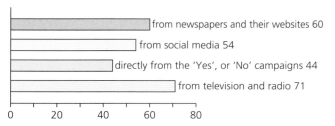

Figure 2.4 **Important sources of information for Scottish voters (%)**
Source: Various polls undertaken September 2014

Key points for and against independence in the 2014 Scottish Referendum

For

Defence The Yes Scotland campaign argued that an independent Scotland would be a member of NATO but without nuclear weapons. Trident nuclear submarines would be removed from Scotland.

NHS The SNP highlighted the further privatisation plans of the UK government and claimed that the NHS was under threat. Sir Harry Burns, former chief medical officer for Scotland, announced that an independent Scotland was necessary to secure the future of the NHS.

Economy and oil Scotland has one of the highest GDPs (14th in the world) and has most of the EU's oil reserves and renewable energy. The present and future revenue from oil would ensure Scotland's economic viability and prosperity. An oil fund similar to that of Norway would be set up to protect Scotland if oil prices were to fall. (Prices fell significantly in the years following the referendum but have made a modest recovery.)

Currency It would be in the best interests of both an independent Scotland and the rest of the UK for Scotland to share the pound and retain the Bank of England as a lender of last resorts to bail out Scottish-based banks if needed. The economy of England would suffer if it excluded an independent Scotland from using the pound.

The EU Scotland would not have to reapply to join the EU as citizens would continue to be EU citizens after a period of negotiation of Scotland's new terms.

National debt Scotland would honour its share of the national debt and would expect to retain the pound. It was not the English pound but the pound of all the nations of the UK.

Against

Defence The Better Together campaign argued that a nuclear-free Scotland would not be granted NATO membership. The removal of Trident would create significant job losses and damage Scotland's economy.

NHS Better Together also argued that as health is a devolved issue Scotland will always be able to protect the NHS from privatisation.

Economy and oil Opponents of Scottish independence argued that the Yes Scotland campaign overestimated the wealth that could be created by North Sea oil. The banking crisis of 2008–10 highlighted the need for Scotland to be part of a larger economy. Public spending per head of population was £12,100 in Scotland and £10,900 for the UK.

Currency The UK coalition government along with the Labour Party ruled out the possibility of a currency union with Scotland. Instead they suggested that Scotland would either have to use the pound in the same way that Panama uses the US dollar, set up a new currency or use the euro.

The EU The UK government argued that if Scotland voted to leave the UK it would have voted to leave an EU member state and would therefore have to reapply as a new member state, relying on the support of governments such as Spain, who would not support such an application.

National debt Alistair Darling maintained that a currency union would not be possible in the event of independence and Scotland could not demand 'the best of both worlds'.

Implications of the 2014 Scottish Independence Referendum

One of the most significant outcomes of the referendum was that the people of Scotland have become better engaged with politics. As Alex Salmond stated after the result was declared: 'Scotland now has the most politically engaged population in western Europe and one of the most engaged in any country, anywhere in the democratic world.' This is likely to have great implications for Scottish politics in the future.

In spite of the result, the referendum guaranteed major changes to the UK's constitutional structure, with immediate calls for an English Parliament from some sections of society and a general consensus on the need for more regional powers to be granted across the UK. Lord Smith of Kelvin assumed responsibility for overseeing a new Scottish Devolution Commission to implement the cross-party decision to give more powers to Scotland.

The referendum result also affected people living in other parts of the Union. The day after the result was declared David Cameron announced that he would use the outcome to implement long-standing Conservative plans to reform Commons rules to stop English MPs being overruled on English-only matters by the votes of Scottish MPs, settling the West Lothian question (see box).

The West Lothian question

The West Lothian question was asked by Tam Dalyell in 1977. It asks why Scottish MPs have the same right to vote at Westminster as any English MP now that large areas of policy are devolved to national parliaments and assemblies in areas such as health, housing, schools and policing.

Figure 2.5 The *Daily Record*, 16 Sep 2014. This vow is credited with persuading some voters who favoured devo-max to reject independence. Opinion polls in 2013–14 indicated that a majority of Scots wanted devo-max. According to Lord Ashcroft's post-referendum poll more than 20 per cent made their decision based on this promise

The implications of EVEL (English votes for English laws)

Critics argue that the decision to prevent Scottish MPs from voting on bills applying only to England (EVEL) will create the situation as described in George Orwell's *Animal Farm* that 'all animals [in this case, MPs] are equal but some animals [MPs] are more equal than others'. It is claimed that Scottish MPs will become second-class parliamentarians and the UK Parliament will become the English Parliament. Critics also point out that only in rare cases have Scottish votes affected legislation that does not apply to Scotland. Between 2001 and 2015 Scottish MPs influenced only 25 of 3,773 votes and most of these affected the entire UK. There is a strong argument that Scottish MPs should not vote on issues such as fox hunting in England. However, with Scotland having greater control over its finances, Conservative MPs wish to exclude Scottish MPS from voting on taxes and budgets. While these bills might at first glance apply to England alone, as they will impact on Scotland's financial situation Scottish MPs claim they should not be classed as English-only bills.

The first use of EVEL occurred in January 2016 when John Bercow, the Commons speaker, certified that large sections of the UK government's Housing and Planning Bill related exclusively to England and would be considered by the new English Grand Committee. Critics of this pointed out that the Conservatives, however, had made use of English Conservative MPs to vote down all the amendments to the Scotland Act supported by almost all Scottish MPs.

Show your understanding

1 Why was the Scottish Referendum described as a triumph for democracy?
2 Which groups in society were mostly likely to favour 'No', and which groups 'Yes', in the Scottish Referendum?
3 Outline the influence of the media during the campaign.
4 Outline the arguments used in 2014 for and against an independent Scotland.
5 What is EVEL and what has been its impact?

The Scotland Act 2016

In November 2015 the Scotland Act finally cleared the House of Commons. Only six hours were devoted to debating more than 800 amendments. The Conservative secretary of state for Scotland, David Mundell, stated that the 'Vow' had now been delivered. He rejected the SNP demand for full fiscal autonomy and for greater powers to be given to the Scottish Parliament. The only important amendment added to the original bill was the Conservative government's adding control of abortion laws to the new powers of the Scottish Parliament. However, all of the SNP amendments for greater powers were rejected, including tax credits, graduate works visa scheme, industrial relations and workers' rights.

In March 2016 the royal assent was granted and the Act became law.

What powers are in the Scotland Act?

- The UK government claimed that this Act made Holyrood the most devolved parliament in the world by granting it total control over income tax and aspects of VAT revenues and welfare.
- From 2017 the Scottish Parliament has had the power to set rates and bands of income tax, keep half of all its VAT receipts, increase welfare payments and create new payments. New welfare powers were claimed to be worth about £2.5 billion. However, Universal Credit has remained a reserved benefit. Mr Mundell denied that this would give the UK government a veto over these new welfare powers.
- The Scottish Parliament is recognised as a permanent part of the constitution, with a referendum required to dissolve it.
- Ministers at Holyrood have control over Scotland's abortion laws.
- Management of the Crown Estate, with the exception of Fort Kinnaird in Edinburgh, has been devolved.
- The Act confirmed the greater borrowing powers for infrastructure spending arising from the Calman Report.

Criticism of the Scotland Act 2016

Critics argue that the allocation of control over income tax only is a poisoned chalice for the SNP. The Scottish government has not been allocated fiscal control over less unpopular taxes such as corporation tax, excise duties, inheritance tax, fuel duties and all VAT revenues. The impact of the massive cuts to public expenditure, including welfare payments, has placed severe pressures on the finances of the Scottish Parliament. Scotland has proportionately fewer high-earning people than England, and the Scottish population is falling relative to that of England. However, it does not have the power to increase immigration (migrants also contribute more in tax than they receive in benefits), which would help to counter the financial burden of an ageing population (see pages 31–32).

What are the options for Scotland's constitutional future?

The main options are as follows:

- Abolition or dilution of the powers of the Scottish Parliament
- A new constitutional arrangement for Great Britain with the possibility of a federal system
- Extension of devolved powers such as devo-max or fiscal autonomy
- Independence

Abolition or dilution of the powers of the Scottish Parliament

The UK Parliament is sovereign and has the right to reduce the powers of the parliaments/assemblies in Scotland, Northern Ireland and Wales. However, the 2016 Scotland Act recognised the permanence of the Scottish Parliament and it can only be abolished if the Scottish people vote for this in a referendum.

The political reality is that there is no real demand by the Scottish people for a referendum on the Scottish Parliament (according to a 2019 poll by market research company Survation, only 14 per cent of Scots favour the abolition of Holyrood). That is not to say, however, that their powers could not be limited at the whim of the UK government. The UKIP Scottish branch supports the abolition of Holyrood and a return to the pre-devolution status of 72 MPs in Scotland and control from London.

Despite being minister for the union, Prime Minister Johnson created a political storm in November 2020 when he stated that devolution was a 'disaster' and 'the biggest mistake' of former Prime Minister Blair. It should not be forgotten that the Conservative party, including Scottish Conservatives, opposed the setting up of a Scottish parliament.

All three devolved parliaments opposed the EU Withdrawal Bill and all refused to approve a consent motion. Their opposition was ignored by the UK Parliament and, in January 2020, the EU Withdrawal Bill became law. This, according to Nicola Sturgeon, displayed 'contempt for devolution'.

The withdrawal of the UK from the EU means that areas such as agriculture and fisheries will no longer be controlled by EU legislation. However, the Conservative government has indicated that the UK will ignore the devolution settlement and retain control of these new 'devolved powers'. The Scottish government has accused the UK government of a 'power grab'. The passing of the UK Internal Market Bill (UIM) has strengthened the view that the powers of the Scottish Parliament are being reduced (see page 12 and box below).

UK Internal Market Bill 2020–21

The UK Internal Market (UIM) refers to the rules that underpin trade across England, Scotland, Wales and Northern Ireland. While the UK was a member of the EU, rules on trading standards, environmental policy and food standards were set by the EU. Part of the UK's annual financial contribution returned to the EU and was used to support, among other things, agriculture, fishing, and infrastructure projects such as new roads. Many of the powers delegated to the EU are part of the powers of the devolved governments of the UK and without UK government legislation would return not to the UK government but to, for example, the Scottish Parliament.

The UK will ignore the devolution settlements and will decide which areas will now be reserved and which will stay devolved, without the agreement of the devolved administrations.

The UK will enshrine in law two principles:

- The principle of mutual recognition
- The principle of non-discrimination

'Mutual recognition means that the rules governing the production and sale of goods and services in one part of the UK are recognised in the other parts of the UK, and should present no barrier to the flow of goods and services between different regulatory systems. Discrimination means that it is not possible for one regulatory regime to introduce rules that discriminate specifically against goods and services from another'. Source: extract from the UIM White Paper, July 2020.

This would not be an issue if the Johnson government aligned with the present EU high standards. However, the government highlights the importance of being able to diverge from EU regulations on goods in order to have the flexibility to sign new trade agreements with non-EU countries; for example, the USA might demand that the UK accept chlorinated chickens (banned in the EU). The UK government wish to ensure that any new international trade agreements will apply to all four nations of the UK. The UK, not the three devolved administrations, will decide which of the new powers will be devolved.

Large-scale state projects will be decided by the UK government and not the devolved governments to ensure conformity and continuity. The UK government might decide to go ahead with a bridge linking Northern Ireland and Scotland without the support of the two devolved administration.

Views of the devolved administrations

All of the three devolved administrations are opposed to the UIM Bill and accuse the UK government of stealing devolved powers by now making them reserved UK powers. Nicola ⇨

Sturgeon stated: 'it is a naked power grab which would cripple devolution … it is a betrayal not just of devolution but of the promises made in the Brexit referendum [of more powers coming to the Scottish Parliament]'. As stated, the UK government will be able to give funding directly for projects which would have previously come from the EU.

The mutual recognition principle threatens the autonomy of Scotland's professional bodies (the Scottish legal profession is exempt). Standards to become a teacher are different in England, for example 'unqualified teacher' is a formally recognised English category. At present the General Teaching Council Scotland (GTCS) can reject applicants to teaching that do not meet their degree professional standards and rigorous programme of teacher training. The UIM will dilute standards, with the GTCS being required to allow 'unqualified teachers' to teach in Scottish schools.

View of the UK government

Westminster officials claim it is more like a 'power-surge' for the Scottish Parliament as it will eventually enable MSPs to be involved with more issues and also point out that more than 60 per cent of Scottish exports go to other home nations. The bill will give the UK government 'the powers to design a UK-wide programme to replace some of the EU programmes'. Westminster officials also argue that the UK government should have the power to make investments in Scotland, Northern Ireland and Wales without the consent of the devolved assemblies.

These types of action by the government in Westminster have led some to question the value of the Sewel Convention (see box).

In April 2021, the UK government further challenged the powers of the Scottish Parliament by refusing to give consent to two bills it had passed. The UK government claimed that these bills (on the rights of children and local government) encroached on Westminster sovereignty. The UK Supreme Court will now decide on either upholding the bills or request Holyrood to amend the bill as requested by the UK government.

Sewel Convention

'The Sewel Convention applies when the UK Parliament wants to legislate on a matter within the devolved competence of the [devolved parliament]. Under the terms of the Convention, the UK Parliament will "not normally" do so without the relevant devolved institution having passed a legislative consent motion.'

Source: www.parliament.uk/site-information/glossary/sewel-convention

A new constitutional arrangement with the possibility of a federal system

The Liberal Democrats have long argued that the UK should adopt a federal system (see box 'Federal system') that would improve the constitutional settlement and could possibly satisfy both unionists and supporters of independence. However, the population dominance of England (England is ten times as populous as Scotland) would make it difficult for the UK to introduce a federal system. As such, the two major political parties, Conservative and Labour, have traditionally been lukewarm towards the concept of federalism. Significantly, various sources suggest that English national identity and support for an English Parliament are strongest in the areas that voted predominantly for Brexit, such as the East and North of England.

After the setting up of the devolved parliaments, Tony Blair, the then Labour prime minister, supported the extension of devolved powers to the regions of England. However, in a range of referenda, the English electorate rejected the creation of regional assemblies.

After Labour's defeat in the 2019 general election, there was significant support among Labour activists for some form of constitutional decentralisation of power, such as the abolition of the House of Lords and the creation of a quasi-federal system. The new Labour leader, Sir Keir Starmer, supports the decentralisation of power in Great Britain.

Extract from a 2019 Labour conference motion

Power must be devolved from Westminster. We should start by building from the ground up with a federal state, starting with the abolition of the House of Lords, replacing it with a fairly elected Senate of the Nations and Regions holding the centre to account.

Source: www.labour.org.uk

Figure 2.6 **Keir Starmer supports the decentralisation of power in the UK**

Federal system

In a federal system, power is divided between a federal (central) government and state/regional governments. Central government is responsible for national issues such as defence and foreign affairs, while the state governments are responsible for everything else, such as law enforcement and taxation. The USA, Canada and Australia are examples of federal systems.

Extension of devolved powers such as devo-max or fiscal autonomy

The vow made by the three leaders of the main political parties in September 2014 to grant significant powers to the Scottish, referred to as devo-max (see page 22), did lead to further powers being granted to the Scottish Parliament, including aspects of social security and taxation. However, this has only led to limited fiscal autonomy and a sharing of social security benefits with the UK Department of Works and Benefits. In 2019–20 the Scottish government spent an additional £35 million to supplement the cuts made by the UK government, thus alleviating poverty in Scotland. It is hoped that all devolved benefits will be administered by Social Security Scotland by the end of 2021.

With the UK leaving the EU, the 2019 request by the Scottish government for immigration to be devolved has been rejected. The Scottish economy has an ageing workforce and so the new immigration laws, which may suit England, may be inappropriate for Scotland (see box 'No to devolved immigration').

No to devolved immigration

In January 2020, the Scottish government presented a 47-page detailed document to the Home Office proposing a 'Scottish visa' to help cope with the end of freedom of movement after Brexit. Under the proposal, the Scottish government would decide on the rules for visas and recommend applicants. The Home Office would security-vet applicants before permitting them to enter the UK, on the condition that they live in Scotland.

Within hours of the submission it was rejected by the UK government. This was interpreted by many commentators as a clear message that Scotland would not be part of the decision making in a post-Brexit world.

Nicola Sturgeon reacted to the curt rejection by stating: 'The end of free movement will harm the whole of the UK – but it will be uniquely harmful for Scotland. It is likely to weaken our economy, damage delivery of our public services and make some of our communities less sustainable.'

Independence

The case for and against independence in 2014 is summarised on page 25. In response to the economic criticisms of independence, the SNP government set up the Sustainable Growth Commission in 2016 to argue the economic case for independence and to consider issues such as a Scottish currency. The report was finally published in May 2018 (see the summary below). First Minister Nicola Sturgeon declared that the report could 'replace the despair of Brexit with optimism about Scotland's future'. However, unionist parties claimed that all it offered Scotland was a decade of austerity and uncertainty.

The Sustainable Growth Commission Report, 2018

Currency

Scotland would have a transition period of using sterling for possibly up to ten years to provide stability and certainty. This would mean that during this period the Bank of England would be in charge of setting interest rates and exchange rate policy; if the economic conditions were right, Scotland might join the euro.

Immigration

Control over immigration would enable the Scottish government to encourage migrants from EU countries to work and stay in Scotland. This would boost the population and address what has been described as 'the demographic timebomb'

(see pages 16–17). There are over 400,000 non-UK-born residents living in Scotland who contribute a net sum of £1.3 billion and pay £4.3 billion in tax and other contributions.

Deficit

It is accepted that Scotland would need to reduce its annual budget deficit, leading to tough spending restrictions. This could be achieved by sensible planning rather than austerity measures. The report accepts that it could take four years to reduce debt to a prudent level.

Public finances

An independent Scotland would have no debt, but would contribute £5.3 billion a year to the UK in an 'annual solidarity payment' as part of its share of UK historic debt. The target set is to raise living standards for Scots to 'equal the best small countries in the world'. Median income in these nations is higher than the average income in Scotland by £4,100 per person.

Banks

A Scottish Central Bank would be set up to hold deposits and act as a limited lender to reduce damage to the wider economy if a bank had some short-term financial shortcomings. A Scottish financial regulator would be created, which would emulate the system south of the border.

Source: 'Scotland – The new case for optimism' report, The Sustainable Growth Commission

Further arguments for and against independence

For independence

- The people of Scotland were told in 2014 that the only way for Scotland to remain in the EU was to reject independence. Despite 62 per cent of Scots voting to remain in the EU, the nation is being forced to leave. As such, the Scottish people should be allowed to hold a second independence referendum to enable them to decide their future. Leaving the EU is a 'material change' and justifies a second referendum.
- Boris Johnson, with 42 per cent of the votes in the 2019 general election, declared that this was a clear mandate from the British public to complete Brexit. In Scotland, the Conservatives fought the 2019 election with the slogan 'No indyref2' and lost six of their seats. In contrast, the SNP, with 45 per cent of the vote, won 80 per cent of Scottish seats and have a democratic mandate to hold a second referendum.
- The new immigration policy is based on the ideology of Brexit and the UK economy will be badly affected. It will have a disastrous impact on Scottish hospitality and care industries and will weaken the Scottish economy. The UK government has refused to allow Scotland to have a say in who can enter the UK. An independent Scotland would work to rejoin the EU and have free movement of EU citizens.

Against independence

- The 2014 independence referendum was 'once in a generation' and the UK now needs to pull together to make Brexit a success. The UK government will not give permission for a second referendum, so any attempt by the Scottish government to agitate for a referendum is a waste of energy and money. The price of oil has fallen and the Scottish economy would be too weak to survive on its own.
- Only 42 per cent of the Scottish public in the 2019 general election voted for the SNP and as such the SNP does not have a democratic mandate to hold a referendum.
- We should be concentrating on fighting the COVID-19 virus pandemic in a united UK.
- The new policies, such as immigration rules, are simply the UK government fulfilling the wishes of the UK public regarding taking control of their borders. The Scottish government should not interfere in an issue that is a reserved power.

Show your understanding

1 Outline the powers granted to the Scottish Parliament by the Scotland Act 2016 and the criticisms made of these powers.
2 Outline the main findings of the 2018 Sustainable Growth Commission.
3 Examine the three possible options for Scotland's constitutional future. Justify which option is the least realistic of the three, and outline the strengths and weaknesses of the other two options.

20-mark question

There are many different opinions about the most effective way to govern Scotland.

Discuss.

Electoral systems

The purpose of elections

In a democracy, citizens can participate freely through voting to elect their representatives.

Elections provide legitimacy to the winning party and to the political system as a whole. By voting, we give consent even if our candidates lose. We can influence the policies of the different parties, and the government of the day will face accountability at the next election.

The failure of the first-past-the-post (FPTP) electoral system to produce a clear winner in the May 2010 and 2017 general elections once again opened the debate over its relevance in the UK in the twenty-first century. As part of the agreement between the Conservatives and Liberal Democrats, in 2010 a referendum was held on whether the alternative vote (AV) system should be adopted (see page 43). Under the agreement, the Conservatives were free to campaign against change. Many critics would have preferred the choice to be between FPTP and a proportional representation (PR) system, rather than AV (a modified version of FPTP).

All the opinion polls prior to the 2015 general election predicted another hung parliament (where the largest party does not have an overall majority in the House of Commons). However, to everyone's surprise, the Conservatives achieved an overall majority, and formed a single party government – FPTP had delivered majority government again!

In 2017, Prime Minister May failed to win an overall majority and had to depend on an agreement with the DUP for a working majority. In 2019, FPTP delivered a comfortable Conservative majority for Boris Johnson.

Figure 3.1 **Voters taking part in the 2019 general election**

In the past, the UK had only one electoral system – FPTP – and this was used to elect MPs to the House of Commons, councillors to local councils across the UK and representatives to the European Parliament.

However, this is no longer the case. As Table 3.1 indicates, a variety of PR systems now operate within the UK for various elections. In Scotland local councillors are elected using the single transferable vote (STV), a form of PR; representatives to the European Parliament were elected using the regional list, also a form of PR; MSPs are elected using the additional member system (AMS), a mixture of FPTP and PR; and finally MPs are elected to the House of Commons using FPTP. So it is no surprise that there is great debate about what system is best for the UK.

Table 3.1 **Electoral systems in use in the UK in 2021**

System	Election of	Constituency type (single- or multi-member)
First-past-the-post (FPTP)	House of Commons Local government Councils in England and Wales (not Scotland)	Single
Additional member system (AMS)	Scottish Parliament Welsh Assembly London Assembly	Single and multi
Regional list	European Parliament 2019 was the last EU election in the UK (not Northern Ireland)	Multi
Single transferable vote (STV)	Scottish local government councils, Northern Ireland Assembly, European Parliament (Northern Ireland only)	Multi

What should an election deliver?

- Should it be a FPTP system that usually helps to deliver a clear winner and strong government, and maintains an effective link between MPs and geographical constituencies?
- Or should it be a PR system that helps to ensure greater proportionality and fairness between votes cast and seats achieved?

First-past-the-post

FPTP is a simple plurality system and is the most important electoral system in the UK because it is used for Westminster general elections. The UK is divided into 650 single-member constituencies, also known as 'seats', and each one elects an MP. The candidate with the most votes becomes the MP.

Table 3.2 illustrates why FPTP is referred to as the 'winner-takes-all' system. In 2017, the SNP candidate won the North-East Fife seat with a majority of only two votes. Similarly, in the 1992 general election 74 per cent of voters in the constituency of Inverness, Nairn and Lochaber did not vote for the winning candidate.

Table 3.2 **North-East Fife general election result 2017**

	Votes	Share (%)
SNP	13,743	32.9
Liberal Democrats	13,741	32.9
Conservative	10,088	24.1
Labour	4,026	9.6

Source: commonslibrary.parliament.uk

There are no prizes for coming second in this system. For example, in the 2015 general election UKIP came second in 120 constituencies and received more than 3.8 million votes. Their reward for such a spectacular performance was one seat in the House of Commons!

Differences in the size of constituencies can reflect geographic factors. The Isle of Wight has the most electors and Na h-Eileanan an Iar (Western Isles) the fewest. Historically, Scotland has been over-represented, and the number of Scottish constituencies was reduced from 72 to 59 in 2005.

Features of FPTP

Maintains a two-party system

FPTP ensures that the proportion of seats won by Conservatives and Labour is far greater than the proportion of votes they receive. In the 2015 general election the combined Conservative/Labour vote was 69 per cent yet they received 85 per cent of the seats (see Table 3.3). Some political commentators argue that FPTP acts as a life-support machine for the two-party system and distorts the will of the electorate.

The figures in bold in Table 3.3 denote the share of the vote of the party that won the most seats in the House of Commons. In 1951 and 1974 the party with the most votes did not win the most seats.

Table 3.3 **The British two-party system, selected years**

| | Share of the vote (%) | | | Share of the seats (%) | | | Liberal / Liberal Democrats | | Overall majority |
	Con	Lab	Con + Lab	Con	Lab	Con + Lab	Votes (%)	Seats (%)	
1951	48.0	**48.8**	96.8	51.4	47.2	98.6	2.5	1.0	17
1974	**37.9**	37.1	75.0	46.6	47.4	94.0	19.3	2.2	–
1983	**42.4**	27.6	70.0	61.0	32.2	93.2	25.4	3.6	144
1992	**41.9**	34.4	76.3	51.6	41.6	93.2	17.9	3.1	21
1997	30.7	**43.2**	73.9	25.0	63.6	88.6	16.8	7.0	179
2010	**36.1**	29.0	65.1	47.2	38.7	85.9	23.0	8.9	–
2015	**36.8**	30.4	67.2	50.1	35.0	85.1	7.9	1.2	12
2017	**42.4**	40.0	82.4	46.0	37.5	83.5	7.4	1.6	–
2019	**43.6**	32.2	75.8	56.1	31.0	87.1	11.6	1.6	80

Source: commonslibrary.parliament.uk

Comfortable government

FPTP usually exaggerates the performance of the most popular party and provides it with a comfortable majority in parliament.

The Conservatives under Margaret Thatcher enjoyed landslide victories in 1983 and 1987, as did Labour under Tony Blair in 1997 and 2001. Again in 2019, the Conservatives under Boris Johnson won with a majority of 80 seats with 43 per cent of the votes.

Unfair to smaller parties

FPTP discriminates against third parties and smaller parties whose support is spread across the UK but is not concentrated in particular regions. The Liberal Democrats have consistently suffered: there are no rewards for coming second in, for example, 300 constituencies. In the 2010 general election, the Liberal Democrats won 23 per cent of the vote but received only 57 seats; in contrast, Labour won 29 per cent of the vote and received 307 seats. In 2015, UKIP and the Green Party received a combined total of 5 million votes, yet only received one seat each.

Limited choice

Many constituencies are safe seats, in which one party has a massive majority over its rivals and is unlikely to lose. For example, all of Glasgow's Westminster constituencies are now held by the SNP, and the Conservatives do badly there. Why should a Conservative supporter make the effort to vote when their vote will be of no consequence? Voters whose favoured party has little support might engage in tactical voting. Instead of voting for their party, electors cast their votes for the candidate best placed to prevent a party they dislike from winning the seat.

Favours parties whose votes are concentrated

The SNP were the clear beneficiaries of having all their votes concentrated in only 59 of the 650 UK constituencies. In 2015 in Scotland the SNP with 50 per cent of the Scottish votes (1.4 million votes) gained 95 per cent of the seats. In contrast UKIP with more than 3.8 million UK votes (12.9 per cent of votes) gained only one seat. In Scotland, UKIP received only 1.6 per cent of the votes (47,000).

Table 3.4 **Average number of votes needed to win a constituency at the 2019 general election**

	Number of votes	
Party	**UK**	**Scotland**
Conservative	38,264	115,489
Labour	50,968	511,838
Liberal Democrats	336,038	65,854
SNP	–	25,882

Source: commonslibrary.parliament.uk

Clearly, in Scotland FPTP now favours the SNP rather than Labour. In the 2010 Scottish results, it only took about 25,000 votes to elect a Labour MP in Scotland; now it is 511,838.

The 2010 general election

In 2010, the Conservatives prevented Labour from winning four general elections in a row, but it was to be no landslide victory for the Conservatives and no breakthrough by the Liberal Democrats.

The most significant feature of the 2010 general election was the failure of FPTP to deliver on its main promise – a single-party government. The last time a hung parliament had occurred was in February 1974.

A total of 326 seats is needed for a party to form a majority government. The Conservative Party achieved only 307 seats and as such formed a coalition government, with David Cameron as prime minister and Nick Clegg (the Liberal Democrat leader) as deputy prime minister. The Conservatives also offered to hold a referendum on the introduction of the AV system to replace FPTP.

The 2015 general election

Despite all the predictions of a hung parliament, David Cameron obtained an overall majority to enable the Conservatives to govern alone – they increased their seats by 24. Gains in the Conservative vote were largely concentrated in the Liberal Democrat seats, and in contrast Labour losses were concentrated in Scotland. The new government's working majority was only 12 and it was predicted that this might create future problems for David Cameron.

It was a strange election that highlighted the inconsistencies and shortcomings of FPTP. Labour increased its percentage of votes but suffered a loss in seats. UKIP gained more than 3.8 million votes but was rewarded with only one seat. In Scotland the unionist parties – Labour, the Conservatives and Liberal Democrats – gained a combined vote of just under 50 per cent of the votes, yet only received 5 per cent of the seats. The Green Party won more than 1 million votes and retained their one seat. It is no wonder the Electoral Reform Society stated that 'this was the most disproportionate result in British election history'. The make-up of parliament clearly demonstrates the massive divide in voting behaviour between Scotland and England.

The distortion between votes cast and seats secured was best illustrated in the results in England and Wales. Here the traditional big three parties won 98 per cent of the available seats.

The 2015 general election witnessed the collapse of support for the Liberal Democrats – in terms of votes UKIP became the third largest party in the UK. The Liberal Democrats lost 49 seats and 5 million voters, and were reduced to a party of eight MPs. Their decision to become junior members of the 2010–15 coalition government condemned the party to near electoral oblivion.

Its leader, former Deputy Prime Minister Nick Clegg, resigned after the election.

The results in Scotland witnessed a tartan tsunami that swept away Labour's dominance and all the traditional theories of voting behaviour. The SNP's number of seats rose from 6 to a staggering 56; in contrast Labour dropped from 40 to 1. The Liberal Democrats lost 10 of their 11 seats to the SNP. The Conservatives witnessed a drop in their electoral support but managed to retain their one seat held by David Mundell, who became the secretary of state for Scotland.

Table 3.5 Result of the 2019 general election: UK turnout 68.7%

Party	Seats	Gain	Loss	Net	Votes	Vote (%)	+/−
Conservative	365	75	9	+66	13,966,565	43.6	+1.2
Labour	202	13	55	−42	12,878,460	32.2	−7.8
SNP	48	14	1	+13	1,454,436	3.9	+0.8
Liberal Democrats	11	3	13	−10	3,696,423	11.6	+4.2
Brexit	0	0	0	0	642,303	2.0	−
Green	1	0	0	0	865,697	2.7	+1.1

Source: commonslibrary.parliament.uk

Table 3.6 Result of the 2019 general election: Scotland turnout 71.1%

Party	Seats	Gain	Loss	Votes	Vote (%)	+/−
SNP	48	14	1	1,242,372	45.0	+8.1
Conservative	6	0	7	717,007	25.1	−3.5
Labour	1	0	6	757,949	18.6	−8.5
Liberal Democrats	4	1	1	219,675	9.5	+2.8

Source: commonslibrary.parliament.uk

Arguments for FPTP

1 It exaggerates the performance of the most popular party, producing a winner's dividend and sometimes a landslide victory. In 1997, Labour won 43 per cent of the vote and gained 419 seats in the House of Commons, giving them a massive majority.

2 Strong single-party government allows the prime minister and cabinet to pursue the policies they stated clearly in their election manifesto without having to compromise with smaller parties in the coalitions associated with PR. The 2015 Conservative manifesto promised a referendum and this took place in 2016.

3 FPTP prevents extremist parties from obtaining representation. The British National Party (BNP) achieved over half a million votes in the 2010 general election but gained no seats. Under a PR system, the BNP won two seats in the 2009 European elections.

4 When an MP retires or dies, a by-election is held to elect a new MP. This enables the public to show their disapproval of a government or a party that has become unpopular.

5 It is easy to understand and implement. Electors only vote once and the results are announced very quickly. In contrast, there were 140,000 spoilt ballot papers in the 2007 Scottish Parliament elections.

Arguments against FPTP

1 The two-party system is past its sell-by date because it no longer reflects voting patterns. In the 1950s, more than 90 per cent of the electorate voted for one of the two major parties; in the 2015 general election, less than 70 per cent of the electorate voted for either the Conservatives or Labour. It is unfair to third and minority parties: in 2015 UKIP received over 3.8 million votes but only received one seat.

2 FPTP does not always produce a victory for the party with the most votes or deliver a fair or decisive result. In the February 1974 election, the Conservatives gained more votes than Labour yet had fewer seats (see Table 3.3). In the 2015 election, the Conservatives formed a government with less than 40 per cent of the votes cast. Again in 2010 and 2017, FPTP failed to deliver a decisive outcome.

3 Strong government does not always create a good or fair government. When FPTP was used in the elections in Northern Ireland, the leader of the Ulster Unionists made the infamous statement 'a Protestant government for a Protestant people'. This abuse of power denied Northern Irish Catholics their civil and political rights. Today in Northern Ireland, under a PR system (STV), there is a power-sharing government between the DUP and Sinn Féin.

4 The winning MP may not have a majority of the votes cast; indeed, they may receive less than 30 per cent of the vote. In 1992, the Liberal Democrat candidate in Inverness East, Nairn and Lochaber won with 26 per cent of the vote.

5 FPTP exaggerates differences and creates division and tension between the nations of the UK. In the 2019 general election, the UK parties in Scotland received over 50 per cent of the votes but received less than 20 per cent of the seats.

The 2017 general election

With the opinion polls giving the Conservatives a 20-point lead over Labour, Prime Minister May decided to go to the polls in the hope of a massive Conservative majority. However, the result of the June election was a disaster for May, and also for UKIP. While the Conservatives were the largest party, they lost their majority in parliament, making it more difficult for May to get her EU legislation through parliament. May's slogan of 'strong and stable leadership' failed to impress the public. She was the only party leader not to take part in the televised debate and, in her limited public campaign appearances, she was often described as appearing ill-at-ease with crowds. In contrast, the Labour leader, Jeremy Corbyn, addressed enthusiastic crowds and came across as an articulate and confident politician, which surprised those who had had low expectations of his performance. Liberal Democrats had hoped that their support for remaining in the EU would win back the voters who deserted them in the 2015 general election. However, increasing their seats from 8 to only 12 was a disappointing result, especially as their percentage of votes was lower than their 2015 performance (7.9 per cent in 2015 compared to 7.4 per cent in 2017). Their leader Tim Farron resigned and was eventually replaced by Jo Swinson.

In Scotland, the Conservative revival – they won 12 new seats from a base line of 1 – enabled Prime Minister May to form a government, albeit with the support of the DUP. Given the outstanding SNP result of 2015, it was to be expected that the support of the SNP would drop in 2017. However, the result stunned the SNP and delighted the unionist parties. The loss of 21 seats and the defeat of key figures such as Angus Robertson (SNP leader at Westminster) and Alex Salmond were bitter blows. Ruth Davidson fighting the election on a 'No indyref2' platform enabled the Conservatives to go from 1 seat to 13 and to restore their support in the south and north-east of Scotland. Labour also witnessed a revival, going from 1 to 7 seats.

The 2019 general election

This election will be remembered as the Brexit election, with traditional social class voting behaviour swept away by the issue of Brexit and national identity. For the fourth general election in a row, the Conservatives emerged as the party with the most seats. More importantly, the Conservatives won with a massive majority of 80 seats. It was a disaster for Labour, with its worst post-war general election performance, and a triumph for the SNP in Scotland. The Conservative slogan of 'Get Brexit Done' had struck a chord with English voters but the Scottish Conservative slogan of 'Stop Indyref2' had failed do the same in Scotland.

The main feature of the election in England was the collapse of Labour support in the Midlands and the north of England. Pro-Brexit Labour-held constituencies – referred to as Labour's red wall – turned Conservative. Tony Blair's seat in Sedgefield was won by the Conservatives by over 4,500 votes – in 1997, Blair had a majority of more than 25,000! Labour lost 59 seats and its share of votes fell from 40 per cent in 2017 to 32 per cent.

The Liberal Democrats did badly, despite increasing their votes. The party's leader Jo Swinson lost her seat in East Dunbartonshire, with the party losing 13 seats and gaining 3. The Greens retained their one MP.

The Scottish public, who voted 62 per cent to remain in the EU, did not endorse Conservative rule. The SNP recovered from their relatively poor 2017 performance by gaining 13 seats and winning 48 of the 59 Scottish seats. The Scottish Conservatives had a disappointing night. The campaign strategy of completely ignoring Brexit and concentrating on opposing a second Scottish referendum led to the loss of 7 of their 13 seats. It was an even greater disaster for Scottish Labour, who lost 6 of their 7 seats, leaving Ian Murray as the sole Labour MP. (The irony was that Corbyn's supporters had tried to deselect him as the Labour candidate.) In Scotland in 2010, under the leadership of Gordon Brown and Iain Gray, Labour won 1 million votes; in 2019, under the leadership of Jeremy Corbyn and Richard Leonard, Labour lost half that number. Labour won only 18.5 per cent of the Scottish votes compared to 34 per cent in England. The Liberal Democrats retained four seats but lost East Dunbartonshire while gaining Fife.

Figure 3.2 The declaration in East Dunbartonshire in 2019: Jo Swinson, leader of the Liberal Democrats, lost her seat by 149 votes to the SNP's Amy Callaghan

Alternative vote

Research by the Electoral Reform Society indicates that the Liberal Democrats would have won an additional 22 seats if AV had been used in the 2010 general election, and 105 more under STV. Table 3.7 indicates what the results would have been under different voting systems in 2019.

Table 3.7 The number of seats won by each party in the 2019 general election under different voting systems

Party	First-past-the-post	Proportional representation (regional list)
Conservative	365	288
Labour	203	216
Liberal Democrats	11	70
SNP	48	28

Source: www.electoral-reform.org.uk

AV is used to elect Australia's lower house, the House of Representatives, and in the UK it is used to elect the leader of the Labour Party and Liberal Democrats. In AV the winning candidate has to achieve an overall majority of the votes cast. Voters write '1' beside the name of their first-choice candidate, '2' next to their second choice and so on. Voters may decide to vote only for their first choice. If no candidate has secured an absolute majority of first preferences, the lowest-placed candidate drops out and the second preferences of his or her votes are transferred to the remaining candidates. If this does not produce a candidate with more than 50 per cent of the votes, the procedure will be repeated until it does.

Arguments for AV

- It would not require any boundary changes and the constituencies would still return one MP.
- All MPs would have gained the majority of the votes and they would have broader support.

Arguments against AV

- The candidate who secures the most first-preference votes may not be elected when second or third preferences have been distributed.
- It retains all the weaknesses of FPTP and is still unfair to third and minority parties.

Alternative vote referendum 2011

The country voted 'No' to changing the electoral system and chose to continue to support a FPTP system that they understood. The Liberal Democrats and the 'Yes' campaign failed to match the impact of the 'No' campaign supported by the Conservative Party and some Labour politicians, such as John Reid. No region had a majority of 'Yes' votes; only in Northern Ireland did the 'Yes' vote muster a respectable figure (see Table 3.8). Of the 440 UK voting areas only ten, including Glasgow Kelvin and Edinburgh Central, voted 'Yes'.

The turnout at the referendum was also low, reflecting the 'Yes' campaign's failure to capture the interest of the public. It was clear that much of the public did not understand the 'alternative vote' (AV) system. Northern Ireland had the highest turnout at 56 per cent, followed by Scotland at 51 per cent. London had the lowest turnout at only 35 per cent.

The Liberal Democrats were also unhappy at the tactics of the 'No' campaign and the Conservative leaders. At the beginning of the campaign David Cameron indicated he would not fight Nick Clegg head to head over the referendum. However, early 2011 opinion polls gave the 'Yes' vote a clear lead, and to placate the right-wingers in his party Cameron threw his weight behind the 'No' campaign.

The prime minister did not disown the blatant lies proclaimed by the 'No' campaign – that new ballot boxes would be needed, that the cost of AV would be astronomical and that a party that came last, such as the BNP, could end up having the winning candidate. However, Labour did not blame the Conservatives for the failed referendum. Labour's Ben Bradshaw tweeted: 'Done countless AV meetings in recent months. Two words sum up the reason for the scale of defeats: Nick Clegg. Toxic. Specially with Labour voters.'

Table 3.8 AV referendum results by UK nation states, May 2011

Nation	Yes (%)	No (%)	Turnout (%)
England	32.1	67.9	42.2
Scotland	36.3	63.6	50.7
Northern Ireland	43.7	56.3	55.8
Wales	34.5	65.4	41.7

Show your understanding

1 Describe the different electoral systems used in the UK.
2 Why is the UK electoral system referred to as first-past-the-post?
3 Refer to Table 3.3. Examine the statements below and indicate to what extent you agree, or disagree, with each:
   a) There has been a significant decline in support for the two major parties.
   b) All elections since 2010 have produced a clear winner.
   c) The Liberal Democrats have been unfairly treated by FPTP.
4 Outline the main features of FPTP and evaluate the arguments for and against PR.
5 Outline the advantages and disadvantages of AV.
6 Analyse the results of the 2011 AV referendum.
7 Describe the results of the 2017 and 2019 general elections.

Proportional representation

Arguments for PR

1 PR is 'fair' because it produces a close correlation between share of the vote and share of seats. The Conservatives received over 22 per cent of the votes and 24 per cent of the seats in the 2016 Scottish Parliament elections.

2 PR gives minor parties more parliamentary representation and encourages voters to vote for them without feeling that their votes will be wasted. In the 2003 elections for the Scottish Parliament, the additional member system (AMS) enabled the Scottish Socialist Party (SSP), the Green Party, the Scottish Senior Citizens Unity Party and the independents to be represented.

3 Coalition government increases the percentage of the electorate supporting the government parties. In the 2010 general election, the coalition Conservative–Liberal Democrat government won a combined 59 per cent of votes.

4 Coalitions encourage consensus, which is the result of compromise. In other words, more voters get some of what they want and less of what they do not want. The Liberal Democrats and Labour formed a coalition government in Scotland in 1999–2007, providing stable and effective government. The UK coalition government of 2010–15 was also regarded as stable and effective.

5 Some people argue that PR will reduce the number of 'wasted votes' and so encourage greater turnout.

Arguments against PR

1 PR can create a government in which a minority party is able to implement its policies. The Liberal Democrats finished fourth in the 2003 Scottish election, yet formed a government with Labour. When they formed a coalition with the Conservatives in May 2010, the Liberal Democrats dropped manifesto pledges such as not increasing student fees.

2 PR can lead to an unstable and weak government. The minority SNP government of 2007–11 found it difficult to implement some of its policies. For example, it failed to implement its policy of minimum pricing of alcohol in November 2010. The minority SNP Government needs the support of the Scottish Greens to get their annual budget through parliament and this gives too much influence to a party with limited electorate support.

3 PR does not always create a more representative Scottish Parliament. In the 2007 Scottish elections, the number of MSPs outwith the four major parties decreased from 17 to 3.

4 Some people argue that AMS creates conflict between the constituency MSP and the seven list MSPs. There is clear rivalry between the two classes of MSPs.

5 The regional list system makes parties more powerful than voters. Being placed first or second on your party's list will mean you have a very good chance of being elected to the Scottish Parliament (assuming you represent one of the major parties). Margo MacDonald, a leading SNP figure, decided to stand as an independent on the Lothian regional list after she had been given a low place on the SNP's party list.

The additional member system

The AMS mixed electoral system has been used to elect the Scottish Parliament and Welsh Assembly since 1999, and also the London Assembly. In Scotland the voters cast two votes. The first vote is to elect the 73 winning candidates in the local constituency elections using FPTP.

Voters also have a second vote in a multi-member constituency, choosing between parties. Scotland is divided into eight regional lists, each electing seven regional list MSPs (see Figure 3.3). The d'Hondt formula is used to ensure that the number of seats for parties in the Scottish Parliament is roughly proportional to the number of votes they won. A party that has a clear lead in the constituency election will do less well in the regional list elections. In 2007 Labour won 37 constituency seats but only 9 regional list seats.

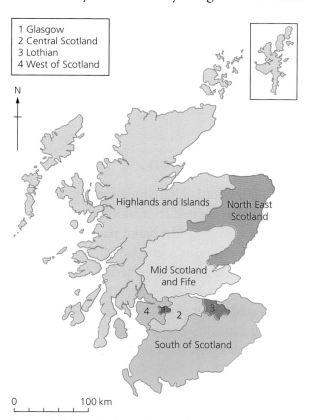

Figure 3.3 **The eight multi-member constituencies in Scotland**

The outcome is that a single party hardly ever wins a majority of seats. AMS ensured the creation of Labour and Liberal Democrat coalition governments after the 1999 and 2003 elections and a minority SNP government after the 2007 election. In 2016 the SNP won 59 constituency seats but only 4 regional list seats. In contrast, Labour won only 3 constituency seats but won 21 regional list seats.

Impact of the Scottish Parliament voting system

AMS, incorporating a strong element of PR, was introduced to reduce the alleged deficiencies of FPTP. What have been the principal consequences of its operation for Scottish politics since 1999?

A fairer result

There is no doubt that AMS increases proportionality by reducing the gap between share of votes and share of seats. In sharp contrast, in 2015 the SNP won 95 per cent of the Scottish seats with only 50 per cent of the votes and in 2019 the SNP won over 80 per cent of the seats with 45 per cent of the votes.

Coalition government or minority-party government

In 1999 and 2003, Labour formed a coalition government with the Liberal Democrats.

In the 2007 election, the SNP overtook Labour as the strongest party in the Scottish Parliament, but only by a single seat. The SNP could not find a coalition partner with enough seats to provide a parliamentary majority. The SNP formed a minority government and had to depend on other parties supporting their policies for the respective bills to be passed in parliament.

Small parties encouraged and sometimes rewarded

In 2003, the Greens and the SSP won 13 out of 56 seats in the second ballot. The presence of Green and SSP MSPs in the Scottish Parliament would not have been achieved under FPTP.

This feature has been erratic in so far as the significant gains of both the Greens and the SSP in 2003 were almost eliminated in 2007, when they lost votes and seats as the SNP surged into first place. Thanks to AMS, the Greens hung on in 2011 with 2 list seats, in 2016 won 6 seats and in 2021 won 8 seats.

Greater voter choice

There has been a large increase in the number of parties and individual candidates competing for seats in the second ballot. No fewer than 23 parties and independents contested the second ballot in both Glasgow and Lothian in 2016.

The second ballot and an increase in the number of parties have given voters the opportunity to vote for more than one party. However, the 2007 and 2011 results emphasise that smaller parties are not guaranteed representation if the battle between the major parties intensifies, meaning that their share of the second-ballot regional vote falls below 5–6 per cent.

Parties rewarded for votes achieved

AMS has maintained the four-party character of Scottish politics by coming to the rescue of the Conservatives. The Conservatives won only one seat in the 2010 general election; in contrast, they had 31 MSPs in the Scottish Parliament of 2016–21.

Can still deliver majority government

The UK-based parties assumed and were happy to accept that AMS would ensure no one party won an overall majority (this would prevent the SNP forming a strong government). However, in 2011 the SNP swept to power with a clear parliamentary majority. In 2021 the SNP won 64 seats, narrowly missing the required 65 seats to achieve a majority government.

Gender representation in the Scottish Parliament

One of the most striking features of the first election to the Scottish Parliament in 1999 was that 48 of the 129 MSPs were women – 37 per cent of the total membership. This was double the proportion of women in the House of Commons and close to the 40 per cent achieved in Sweden. In both the 2011 and 2016 elections, 45 women MSPs were elected.

However, the gap has significantly closed since. In the 2020 UK Parliament, there were a record number of female MPs: 220. This equals 34 per cent of MPs. In 2021, 58 women were elected to the Scottish Parliament – 45 per cent of the total membership.

Electorate confusion

The May 2007 Scottish Parliament and local council elections created confusion among the electorate. A change to the ballot papers for the parliamentary elections and a switch from FPTP to STV for local council elections seemed to confuse some voters. In the 2003 elections there had been 45,700 rejected ballot papers; in the 2007 elections, a staggering 140,000 were rejected. This was not an issue in the subsequent 2011 and 2016 elections.

Scottish Parliament election, May 2011

Alex Salmond's landslide victory took everyone by surprise. In January 2010 early opinion polls gave Labour a clear 16 points lead. This was confirmed in the 2010 general election when Scottish Labour easily dismissed the SNP challenge and, in fact, Scotland was the only part of the UK where Labour's vote increased.

When the Scottish Parliament elections came around in May 2011, the SNP gained 22 seats and achieved what was regarded as impossible under the proportional voting system – an overall majority of seats: 69 out of 129. In the north-east, the SNP won all 10 constituency seats, and still obtained another on the regional list. The results were all the more remarkable given that in the 1999 election the then-dominant Labour Party achieved only 56 seats.

Scottish voters punished the Liberal Democrats for their coalition with the Conservatives in Westminster and the party was reduced from 16 MSPs to 5. Overall the party's vote slumped below half its 2007 level with Liberal Democrat disaffected voters switching to the SNP. It was also a disappointing result for the Conservatives and a slight disappointment for the Greens. Conservative support fell to its lowest level in Scotland and the party lost two of its MSPs. The number of Green MSPs did not increase after the election but they were able to retain their two MSPs.

Table 3.9 **Summary of total MSPs by party from 2003 to 2016**

Party	2003	2007	2011	2016
SNP	27	47	69	63
Labour	50	46	37	24
Conservative	18	17	15	31
Liberal Democrats	17	16	5	5
Green	7	2	2	6
SSP	6	0	0	0
Others	4	1	1	0

Scottish Parliament election 2016

As predicted the SNP won a third election in a row, with 63 seats, but just failed to win an overall majority. The d'Hondt system, designed to prevent the winning party gaining an overall majority, had worked. However, what was not predicted was the Conservative Party pushing Labour into third place.

The SNP increased its votes and seats in the constituency results. The SNP vote was up 1.1 per cent on 2011, winning 59 of Scotland's 73 FPTP seats, an increase of 6. It narrowly missed being higher – the SNP just failed to win Dumbarton and Edinburgh Southern. This would have given the SNP an overall majority. As it was, the d'Hondt regional list system punished the SNP for gaining over a million constituency votes and 80 per cent of the constituency seats. Despite gaining almost 940,000 regional votes, the SNP received only 4 regional seats; in 6 of the 8 regions, the SNP got no list MSPs (in contrast, the Conservatives with 524,000 regional votes won 24 regional seats).

Under the leadership of Ruth Davidson (her name was placed on the ballot papers), the Conservatives played the unionist card and claimed that they were the only party that could effectively provide a strong opposition to the SNP and defend the Union.

For Labour, their electoral nightmare continued. The party that had once dominated Scottish politics was completely humiliated, with the 'despised' Tories taking second place. In 1999, Labour won 56 seats, yet 17 years later that number had been reduced to just 24. In an election where polls indicated that 90 per cent of 'Yes' voters would back the SNP, Labour had a straight battle with the Conservatives for the 'No' voters. The Tory message was clear – total opposition to a second referendum and no tax rises.

In terms of the minority parties, the Greens received six seats, pushing the Liberal Democrats into fifth spot. Yet while the combined constituency and list votes for the Liberal Democrats added up to just under 300,000, it was the Greens with a combined vote of about 160,000 who gained the most seats, which brought into question the fairness of the AMS system. The Liberal Democrats had at least retained their five seats, and its leader, Willie Rennie, won a constituency seat (in contrast, Kezia Dugdale failed to win her constituency seat).

Table 3.10 Scottish Parliament election results May 2016

Party	SNP	+/−	Lab	+/−	Cons	+/−	Lib Dem	+/−	Green	+/−
Total seats	63	−6	24	−13	31	+16	5	−	6	+4

Scottish Parliament election 2021

The SNP won a historic fourth election, winning 62 of the 73 constituency seats (over 80 per cent) under FPTP. However, gaining three constituency seats ensured that under the d'Hondt system the SNP with over a million regional votes achieved only two regional MSPs. As such, the SNP lost two of their regional seats and ended up with an overall total of 64 – one short of a majority. The Conservatives retained their second place with 23 per cent of the regional list votes. The AMS system clearly rewarded the Conservatives, who won 26 regional list seats, which is 40 per cent of the regional list seats. The system gave them a higher proportion of the seats than the proportion of the votes that they had won. The election witnessed the highest turnout for a Scottish parliamentary election – 63.5 per cent.

The SNP increased its votes and seats in the constituency results. The SNP vote was up 1.2 per cent on 2016, winning 62 of Scotland's 73 FPTP seats, an increase of three. It narrowly missed being higher – the SNP just failed to win Dumbarton and Edinburgh Southern. This would have given the SNP an overall majority. As it was, the d'Hondt regional list system punished the SNP for gaining over a million constituency votes and 80 per cent of the constituency seats. Despite gaining over a million regional votes, the SNP received only two regional seats. Tactical voting played an important part in preventing an even greater SNP victory. A website set up by a pro-UK campaign encouraged voters who opposed a second independence referendum to put in their postcode and find out which unionist political party they should vote for to prevent an SNP constituency victory.

The Conservatives once again played the unionist card and claimed that they were the only party that could effectively provide a strong opposition to the SNP and defend the Union. Their new leader, Douglas Ross, concentrated totally on the constitutional issue. Once again, the Conservatives had clearly outmanoeuvred Labour. In 2011 the Conservatives won only 15 seats; ten years on they had more than doubled to 31 seats. Although the Conservatives lost two constituency seats, they managed to win a further two regional list seats with a slight increase in their overall votes.

For Labour, their electoral nightmare continued. The party that had once dominated Scottish politics fell further behind the Conservatives. Labour lost one of its three constituency seats but managed to retain Dumbarton. Labour's new Scottish leader, Anas Sarwar, achieved a high personal approval rate. His attempt to focus on non-constitutional issues, as well as the Conservative's encouragement to vote Conservative in the regional list vote to prevent a second referendum, ensured that Labour won their fewest ever seats in the Scottish Parliament, declining from 24 to 22.

In terms of the minority parties, the Greens received eight regional list seats, an increase of two, giving the pro-independence parties a clear majority with a total of 72 seats. The Liberal Democrats retained four of their five constituency seats but were badly served by the d'Hondt system. Despite receiving over 137,000 regional list votes, the Liberal Democrats ended up with no regional list MSPs. In contrast the Greens, with over 220,000 votes, won eight regional list seats. Alba, the new independence party, won no seats. Its leader, Alex Salmond, had urged independence supporters to vote SNP in the constituency seats and Alba in the regional list to create a 'supermajority'. Mr Salmond had warned that a second SNP vote in the regional list would be a wasted vote. In this context he was correct. With over a million regional list votes, the SNP only won two seats.

Table 3.11 **Scottish Parliament election results May 2021**

Party	SNP	+/–	Lab	+/–	Cons	+/–	Lib Dem	+/–	Green	+/–
Total seats	64	+1	22	–2	31	–	4	–1	8	+2

Table 3.12 **Scottish Parliament election May 2021 constituency results**

Party	Seats	+/–	Votes	%	+/– %
SNP	62	+3	1,291,214	47.7	+1.2
Labour	2	–1	574,393	21.6	–1.0
Conservative	5	–2	591,978	21.9	–0.1
Liberal Democrats	4	–	187,806	6.9	–0.9
Green	0	–	34,990	1.3	+0.7

Table 3.13 **Scottish Parliament election May 2021 regional list results**

Party	Seats	+/–	Votes	%	+/– %
SNP	2	–2	1,094,374	40.3	–1.4
Labour	20	–1	485,819	17.9	–1.2
Conservative	26	+2	637,131	23.5	+0.6
Liberal Democrats	–	–1	137,152	5.1	–0.1
Green	8	+2	220,324	8.1	+1.5

Table 3.14 Scottish Parliament election May 2021 parliamentary region results

Region	SNP	Labour	Conservative	Liberal Democrats	Green
Highlands and Islands	1	1	4	–	1
North East Scotland	–	2	4	–	1
Mid Scotland and Fife	–	2	4	–	1
Central Scotland	–	3	3	–	1
Lothian	–	2	3	–	2
Glasgow	–	4	2	–	1
West of Scotland	–	3	3	–	1
South of Scotland	1	3	3	–	–
Total	2	20	26	–	8

National/regional party list

This party-list PR system was introduced for elections to the European Parliament in England, Scotland and Wales (but not in Northern Ireland) in 1999. Here the electorate does not vote for individual candidates but for a party. Political parties draw up a national or regional list of candidates in the order in which they will be elected. Representatives are elected from 11 large multi-member regions, each electing between 3 and 10 MEPs. In the 2019 European election, Scotland elected 6 MEPs (see Table 3.15).

In May 2014, the UK elected 72 MEPs (59 from England) to the European Parliament, with Nigel Farage, the leader of the Brexit Party, winning the most votes and seats.

The 2019 European Parliament elections came after Prime Minister Theresa May tried three times to secure MPs' backing for her Brexit plan and had announced her resignation. Farage, the former leader of UKIP, helped to form the Brexit Party to contest the European election. His party won 29 seats while the pro-EU Liberal Democrats came second, with 16 seats. It was a disaster for the Conservatives and Labour, with the former winning less than 10 per cent of the vote.

While Scotland followed some of the national trends, it had its own political dimension. The SNP once again had the most votes. It increased its representation to three MEPs, an increase of one. Labour did badly, losing its two MEPs while the Conservatives retained their seat. The Brexit Party replaced UKIP for the last remaining Scottish seat.

Summary of the 2019 European elections

- Turnout was just below 37 per cent – the second highest in any European election in the UK.
- The Brexit Party received the highest share of the vote in 9 of the 12 regions – with 32 per cent overall.
- The Conservative Party was in fifth place.
- The Liberal Democrats took second place with 20 per cent of the vote.
- The Labour Party fell to third place overall, with less than 15 per cent of the vote.
- The Green Party also made gains, seeing its best performance since 1989.
- Newly formed Change UK did not win any seats, while UKIP lost significant support to the Brexit Party.

Advantages of the regional list

- There is greater proportionality between votes cast and seats gained. In the 2004 European elections, which used FPTP, Labour gained 44 per cent of the vote and received 74 per cent of the seats.
- It rewards smaller parties. In the 2009 European elections, UKIP won 16.5 per cent of the vote and received 13 seats (the same as Labour).

Disadvantages of the regional list

- The link between representatives and constituents is weakened in large multi-member constituencies. Very few people in Scotland could name their MEP.

Table 3.15 **European election results, 2019: Scotland**

Party	Votes		MEPs (total)
	Total	**%**	
SNP	594,533	37.8	3
Labour	146,724	9.3	–
Conservative	182,476	11.6	1
Liberal Democrats	218,285	13.9	1
Green	129,603	8.2	0
Brexit Party	233,006	14.8	1

Single transferable vote

The STV PR system was used in the Scottish local government elections for the first time in May 2007. It is also used in Northern Ireland for elections to both the Northern Ireland Assembly and the European Parliament.

The main features of STV are:

1 Representatives are chosen from multi-member constituencies. In a five-member local government constituency (ward), voters rank their preferences among the candidates using the figures 1–5. Often the number of candidates will be in double figures.
2 Electors can vote for as many or as few candidates as they like.
3 A complicated quota system is used to calculate the minimum number of votes required to win one of the seats. The quota is calculated by dividing the number of votes cast by the number of seats available plus one. In a four-member constituency where 150,000 votes were cast, a candidate would require 30,001 votes in order to be elected. Any votes in excess of this quota are redistributed on the basis of second preferences.

The Local Governance (Scotland) Act (2004) facilitated this change from the traditional FPTP system to a form of PR. It resulted in substantial change in both the composition and political control of Scottish local authorities.

Scottish local government elections 2012 and 2017

The introduction of the STV system in 2007 has led to a fairer distribution of seats among the parties. However, it is now more difficult for one party to gain overall control of a council and this means that most councils have a coalition administration. In 2006, 13 councils were controlled by Labour and one by the SNP; after the 2017 local government elections no council was controlled by the four main Scottish parties.

In the 2017 election, the Conservative revival resulted in their coming second place to the SNP

(Conservatives returned 276 seats compared to 431 for the SNP). Labour did badly, losing 133 seats and their control of Glasgow, but took comfort from the SNP's failure to win a majority in any of the councils.

Table 3.16 **2017 local council election results**

Party	Number of councillors	Net gain/loss compared with 2007 elections
SNP	431	−7
Scottish Labour	262	−133
Scottish Liberal Democrats	67	−3
Scottish Conservative	276	+164
Scottish Green	19	+5

Source: www.electoralcommission.org.uk

Table 3.17 **Councils controlled by Labour, SNP, Independents**

Party	2003 (FPTP)	2007 (STV)	2012 (STV)
Labour	13	4	0
SNP	1	2	0
Independents	6	4	4
Total councils	20	10	4

Source: www.electoralcommission.org.uk

Show your understanding

1 Describe briefly how AMS works in Scotland.
2 AMS ensures a fairer distribution of seats and a greater choice for the electorate. To what extent did the 2007 and 2011 Scottish Parliament elections achieve this outcome?
3 Describe how the national/regional party list system operates and its impact on the political parties in the 2014 and 2019 European elections.
4 Describe briefly how the STV system operates.
5 Outline the impact of STV on the Scottish local council elections of 2012 and 2017.

Developing your skills

To what extent were the 2016 and 2021 Scottish Parliament elections a triumph for the SNP and a disappointment for all the other parties?

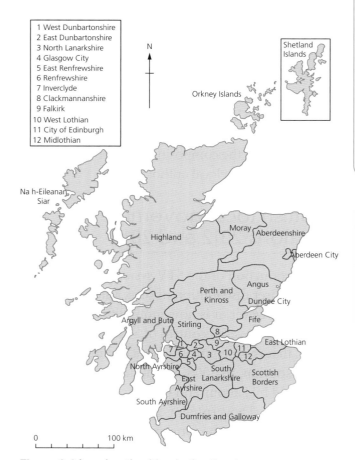

1 West Dunbartonshire
2 East Dunbartonshire
3 North Lanarkshire
4 Glasgow City
5 East Renfrewshire
6 Renfrewshire
7 Inverclyde
8 Clackmannanshire
9 Falkirk
10 West Lothian
11 City of Edinburgh
12 Midlothian

Figure 3.4 **Local authorities in Scotland**

4 Voting behaviour

The study of voting behaviour – the ways in which the public decide which political party to vote for – is a complex issue. Which party an individual votes for is influenced by long-term factors such as socio-economic background (often and traditionally referred to as social class), age, national identity, ethnic and religious background, and region; and by short-term factors such as governing competence, the state of the economy and the popularity of the respective parties' leaders and policies.

Political scientists have developed theories of voting behaviour to explain the interaction between the electorate and their voting preferences. They can be divided into long-term and short-term influences, as follows:

Long-term influences

The main theories are the sociological and party identification models, which focus on the social characteristics of voters – especially social class. In recent times the rise of Scottish and English national identities appears to have weakened the influence of social class.

Short-term influences

The main theory is the rational choice model, which focuses on the significant factors pertaining to a particular issue. The major issue in 2017 and 2019 was the 2016 decision to leave the EU – Boris Johnson's slogan in England and Wales was to 'Get Brexit Done'. A second factor was the unpopularity of Jeremy Corbyn among the general public.

Long-term factors were considered to be the most important influence on voting behaviour in the period 1945–78. This was the era of party identification, class alignment and two-party dominance. The period between 1979 and the present day is described as one of declining party identification and partisan de-alignment. Short-term factors such as the image of party leaders and the state of the economy are now considered to have a much greater influence on voting behaviour.

Class voting and partisanship

Until the late 1980s, social class was regarded as the dominant influence in voting behaviour. P.J. Pulzer, the Oxford political scientist, stated in 1967: 'Class is the basis of British party politics; all else is embellishment and detail.'

Most people voted for the party that best represented the interests of their social class. A large majority of the working class voted for the Labour Party, while much of the middle class supported the Conservatives. Ideologically, Labour was a socialist party. It stood for a redistribution of wealth in society in order to reduce major differences between the rich and poor. Labour believed that large industries, especially the utilities like gas and electricity, should be owned by the state. In contrast the Conservatives emphasised less state interference and believed in leaving most economic decision making in the hands of the market economy, while accepting the welfare state.

The vast majority of the electorate voted for one of the two major parties: in the 1951 general election 97 per cent of the electorate voted either Conservative or Labour. This continuity in voting patterns reflected long-term feelings of positive attachment to one of the main parties (partisanship). This distinct party identification, similar to attachment to a football club, was passed down from generation to generation. However, both class voting and partisanship have declined since the 1970s. The 2015 election result in Scotland witnessed the complete collapse of class voting, with national identity becoming the dominant factor. In the 2019 election the issue of Brexit, along with an apparent rise of English nationalism, had disastrous consequences for Labour as traditional Labour voters, frustrated with the party's position on Brexit, lent their vote to the Conservatives instead.

Party membership

The general trend of people being less strongly affiliated to parties is reflected in the decreasing number of party members:

- Conservative membership peaked at about 2.8 million members in the 1950s, but had fallen to 180,000 by 2019.
- In the same period Labour membership fell from about 1.1 million in the 1950s to 187,000 by 2014. The election of Corbyn as party leader led to a significant rise in membership – to 485,000 in 2019.

- As a result of the Scottish referendum, membership of the SNP surged from just under 26,000 to more than 125,000, making the SNP the UK's third largest party.
- The result of falling membership is a large and growing number of floating voters, especially the young, with falling turnout and no lasting loyalty to any party.

Source: commonslibrary.parliament.uk

What is social class?

Social class is defined by social and economic status. The term 'working class' has traditionally been used to refer to people in manual occupations and 'middle class' to those in non-manual employment.

The market research definition of class structure uses six categories:

- Categories A, B and C1 are the non-manual middle class.
- Categories C2, D and E constitute the manual working class.

Figure 4.1 **A category A worker**

Figure 4.2 **A category C2 worker**

Partisan de-alignment

The changing trends in social class and voting have been explained by leading social scientist, Professor Ivor Crewe (see fact file). The result of his analysis can be seen in the decline in the number of voters who identify strongly with either Labour or the Conservatives. In 1961, 44 per cent of voters were 'very strong' supporters of one of the main parties, but by 2010 this figure had dropped to only 12 per cent. The core vote for the two main political parties has declined significantly, so parties now have to work harder to win over floating voters who do not have strong allegiances and switch their votes from election to election. This explains why in the 1980s the Conservatives gained support from the working class. In the 1974 general election only 26 per cent of the skilled working class (C2) voted Conservative; in 1987, 40 per cent voted Conservative. The Conservative governments of the 1980s tapped into the aspirations of this new upwardly mobile, skilled working class through policies such as the sale of council houses, lower taxation and the opportunity for ordinary workers to buy shares in newly privatised industries such as gas and electricity.

New Labour, under the leadership of Tony Blair, was determined to modernise the Labour Party by ending its commitment to socialism. New Labour offered the 'third way' by appealing to the middle classes and becoming a catch-all party through low taxation, increased NHS spending and attractive social policies such as the introduction of the minimum wage. Labour retained its gains among middle-class voters in 2001 and 2005 but its working-class vote fell. When he became Conservative leader, David Cameron copied Tony Blair and modernised his party. This enabled the Conservatives to win both the 2010 and 2015 general elections.

Fact file

The de-alignment explanation

De-alignment means a weakening relationship between social class and party support – a decline in the class basis of UK politics. Ivor Crewe argued that the distinction between social classes had been eroded by changes in the labour market (the decline of heavy industry), the increase in female workers, greater affluence and improved access to higher education. Crewe divided the working class into two groups: the old working class and the new working class, who aspire to be middle class.

Features of the old working class:
- unskilled manual occupation in traditional heavy industries
- trade union membership
- living in a council house
- located in greater numbers in the north of England, Wales and Scotland.

Features of the new working class:
- more likely to be skilled with better qualifications
- owner-occupiers, many having bought their council house under the Conservative policy of right to buy
- working in new high-tech industries
- found in greater number in the southern half of England.

The 2015 election share of votes indicates that UKIP's main support came from classes C2, D and E. A 2013 poll indicated that the top priority for working-class voters was reducing immigration – immigration control was one of the top policy aims of UKIP. It is too early to state whether the collapse of Labour votes in Labour's heartland of northern England during the 2019 general election marks the end of traditional social-class voting.

Table 4.1 **Class voting, selected years (share of the vote, %), 2015 result refers only to England and Wales**

	Middle class (ABC1)	Skilled working class (C2)	Unskilled working class (DE)	Middle class (ABC1)	Skilled working class (C2)	Unskilled working class (DE)
	Conservative			Labour		
1979	59	41	34	24	41	49
1997	39	27	21	34	50	59
2010	39	37	31	27	29	40
2015	43	32	27	27	32	41
2017	44	47	41	40	40	44
2019	43	49	47	33	31	34

Source: Various polls

Geography/regional differences

There have traditionally been clear regional variations in voting in Britain. A 'North–South' divide has usually been evident, with Labour support highest in the north of England, Scotland (prior to the 2015 election), Wales and large urban areas and council-house schemes; the Conservatives typically do best in southern England, and in English suburbs and rural areas. These geographical divisions in voting patterns in England and Wales can be explained in part by social-class factors. Labour's safe seats tend to be in inner-city constituencies in cities such as Manchester and Liverpool. In contrast, Conservative safe seats tend to be in prosperous English constituencies in the suburbs and rural areas. However, the outcome of the 2019 general election in England, with the collapse of Labour votes in the north of England, reflects the decline in social-class voting in England and Wales.

Table 4.2 **Regional voting, 2019 general election**

	Conservative	Labour	Liberal Democrats
Overall			
Share of the vote (%)	43.6	32.9	11.8
Seats	365 (+48)	202 (−60)	11 (−1)
By region (share of the vote, %)			
North-East	38.3	42.6	6.8
Yorkshire and the Humber	43.1	38.9	8.1
North-West	37.5	46.5	7.9
West Midlands	53.4	33.9	7.9
East Midlands	54.8	31.7	7.8
London	32.9	48.1	14.9
South-East	54.0	22.1	18.2
South-West	52.8	23.4	18.2
Scotland	25.1	18.6	9.5
Wales	36.1	40.9	6.0

Source: commonslibrary.parliament.uk

The end of social-class voting in Scotland?

In the 2010 general election, Labour had actually increased its votes and won back the two by-election seats it had lost during the 2005–10 parliament. The political consensus even after the SNP victory in the 2011 Scottish Parliament elections was that in UK elections the Scottish electorate would remain loyal to Labour.

Prior to the 2014 Scottish Independence Referendum, the unionist parties expected an easy win as opinion polls suggested that only between a quarter and a third of Scots supported independence. Scottish Labour hoped that this would demoralise the SNP and their supporters, leading to Labour's dominance again in the 2015 general election in Scotland. The reality was the opposite.

The referendum unleashed an exceptional level of public engagement and a surge in support for the SNP. Nationalism had replaced social class as the dominant voting factor in Scotland (in England and to a lesser extent in Wales, UKIP played a British/English national identity card with policies hostile to immigrants and to EU membership). Moreover Scottish Labour's alliance with the Conservatives in the Better Together campaign would have the same dire electoral effect as that experienced by the Scottish Liberal Democrats in the 2011 Scottish Parliament elections. It was Scottish Labour that experienced internal turmoil and demoralisation. Its leader, Johann Lamont, resigned in October 2014, claiming that the Scottish Labour Party was 'just a branch office of London'. In contrast the resignation of the SNP leader, Alex Salmond, led to the triumphant coronation of Nicola Sturgeon as party leader. Jim Murphy, a Scottish Labour MP, was elected leader of Scottish Labour.

The results of the 2017 and 2019 general elections confirmed the end of Labour dominance in Scotland. In terms of social-class voting, the SNP support came almost equally from all sections of society.

The end of social-class voting in England?

The results of the 2019 general election followed the same trend that Scotland has experienced since 2015, with a massive decline in traditional social-class voting. As indicated, voting in 2019 was based on two connecting issues – the public's perception of Corbyn's leadership and

---

Show your understanding

1 Outline the long-term and short-term influences on voting behaviour.
2 Outline the evidence that supports the view that social class was once regarded as being the most important factor in voting behaviour.
3 Explain the term 'partisan de-alignment' and describe its impact on voting behaviour.
4 a) Refer to Table 4.1. To what extent was social class a significant influence in voting behaviour between 1979 and 2015 in England and Wales?
   b) What evidence suggests that, in the general elections of 2017 and especially 2019, social-class influence in voting behaviour significantly declined?
5 Why has the influence of social class declined in England and Wales?
6 Refer to Table 4.2. What conclusions can be drawn regarding the voting patterns across the regions and nations of Great Britain in 2019?

Brexit. However, the long-term factor – the growth of English nationalism – also played its part. In opinion polls on identity, the areas where the majority regarded themselves as English and not British were also the areas that supported Brexit in the 2016 referendum.

Other social factors

Age

There are clear links between age and party support, and the gap has widened in recent elections (see Table 4.3). In general elections from the 1980s to the 2000, the over-65s were around one-third more likely to vote Conservative than were those aged 18–24. By 2015, they were two-thirds more likely. This group did not suffer from the austerity cuts of 2010–19, with for example their state pensions being safeguarded by the triple lock protection of the value of the state pension (annual pensions will increase either by 2.5 per cent or by the rate of inflation or earnings). In the last five elections in England and Wales, Labour outperformed the Conservatives among those aged 18–24 (56 per cent to 21 per cent in the 2019 general election). In contrast, older groups have consistently favoured the Conservative Party; in the age group 60–69 the Conservative figure in 2019 was 57 per cent compared to the Labour figure of 22 per cent (see Table 4.4). It should be noted that the growing number of older people are more likely to vote than the young and this is advantageous to the Conservatives. In the 2019 general election, turnout for those under 25 was only 47 per cent; in contrast, for those over 65 it was 74 per cent. The older generation also played a key role in ensuring a 'Leave' vote in the 2016 EU Referendum. In Scotland, the SNP support was stronger among the under 50s and weakest in the 65+ age group.

Table 4.3 **Percentage of age group voting Conservative at general elections: selected years**

Year	Age 18–24	Age 65+
1987	38	48
1997	28	38
2005	29	42
2015	26	48
2017	21	62
2019	21	62

Source: Various polls

Table 4.4 **Age and voting (%), 2019 general election**

	Conservative	Labour	Liberal Democrats
Overall			
Share of the vote (%)	45	33	12
By age (share of the vote, %)			
18–24	21	56	11
25–29	23	54	12
30–39	30	46	14
40–49	41	35	13
50–59	49	28	12
60–69	57	22	11
70+	67	14	11

Source: Various polls, 2019

Education

The educational status of voters was an important dividing line in how people voted in England and Wales. Those who had an undergraduate or higher degree were far more likely to vote Labour than Conservative, a staggering 43 per cent to 29 per cent (see Table 4.5). This reflects the voting patterns of the 2016 referendum, where voters with higher educational qualifications voted to stay in the

EU, and this likely explains why, for this group, the Conservative vote was so low, given their slogan of 'Get Brexit Done'. In Scotland, the lowest support for the SNP came from those with fewer or lower educational qualifications.

Table 4.5 **Vote by education level (%), 2019 general election**

Level	Conservative	Labour	Liberal Democrats	SNP
Low (GCSE or below)	58	25	8	3
Medium	48	31	11	4
High (degree or above)	29	43	17	4

Source: Various polls, 2019

Gender

Until the 1997 general election women were more likely to vote Conservative than men. However, since then more women than men have voted Labour. According to polls, in the 2019 general election, 35 per cent of women voted Labour compared to only 31 per cent of men. However, the gender gap among Conservative voters overall is very small – among men, 46 per cent and among women, 44 per cent. Similarly to the general age pattern, women under the age of 50 favoured Labour. Among women under 25 the difference was significant – only 15 per cent favoured the Conservatives compared to 65 per cent for Labour. In contrast, older women favoured the Conservatives – in the 65+ group by a massive 64 per cent to 18 per cent. Given that in this age group there are more women than men, this again is advantageous for the Conservatives.

Table 4.6 **Gender and voting (%), 2019 general election**

	Conservative	Labour	Liberal Democrats
Men	46	31	12
Women	44	35	11

Source: Various polls, 2019

Ethnicity

Voters belonging to a minority ethnic group are traditionally far more likely to vote Labour and far less likely to vote Conservative. In the 2015 election two out of every three Black, Asian, and minority ethnic (BAME) voters supported Labour. Not surprisingly, given UKIP's anti-immigration policies, it received very little support from BAME voters. In both the 2017 and 2019 general elections, this pattern of voting was maintained. Widely publicised complaints of anti-Semitism in the Labour party led to many British Jews not voting for Corbyn's Labour Party.

Table 4.7 **Vote by ethnic grouping (%), 2019 general election**

Group	Conservative	Labour	Liberal Democrats	Others
White voters	48	29	12	11
All BAME voters	20	64	12	4

Source: Ipsos MORI 2019

Electoral turnout

The 2019 general elections saw turnout decrease slightly from 68.8 per cent to 67.3 per cent (well below the post-war average of 78 per cent). In contrast, voting turnout increased in Scotland from 66.4 per cent to 68.1 per cent. The decrease in voting turnout can partially be explained by some Labour voters in the north of England who, unhappy with Corbyn and his Brexit policy, but unwilling to vote for the Conservatives, decided not to vote at all. In Scotland, the Tory demand of 'Get Brexit Done' was unpopular and probably explains the rise in SNP support.

Apathy and disillusionment

It is clear that in recent years there has been a trend of growing dissatisfaction with the political parties and Westminster politics, which has led to a lower turnout. As stated, the proportion of the public who have a strong attachment to a political party has declined (although membership of the SNP and Labour, under Jeremy Corbyn, increased). The 2009–10 MPs expenses scandal further eroded public confidence and created greater disillusionment. The Electoral Reform Society describes FPTP as 'a voting system in crisis' and stated that 'nearly half a million people signed petitions calling for electoral reform in the fortnight after the [2015] election'. In the 2019 general election, in the south-east of England, the Conservatives won 74 of the 84 seats (just under 90 per cent) with only 54 per cent of the votes. The situation in Scotland was considered by some parts of the electorate to be even more unfair: the SNP won 81 per cent of the Scottish seats with 45 per cent of the vote.

Social groupings

Clearly social factors influence turnout. Those traditionally categorised as middle class, as well as university-educated individuals, older people and those living in rural areas are most likely to vote. People aged over 60 are almost twice as likely to vote as those aged 18–24.

1 To what extent is there a 'North–South divide' in voting behaviour? You should refer to Table 4.2 in your answer.
2 Why can it be argued that the 2015 general election in Scotland marked the end of social-class voting in Scotland?
3 Why can it be argued that the 2017 and 2019 general elections marked the end of social-class voting in England?
4 Why has age become a more important factor in voting behaviour in recent elections?
5 Assess the influence of education, ethnicity and gender on voting behaviour.

Short-term influences

The rational choice model considers the impact of short-term factors that influence the choice made by individual voters at elections. With the decline in party identification there is a growing number of floating voters who are undecided prior to a general election. They will be influenced by a range of issues such as the policies of the parties, the image of the party leader, the state of the economy and even by which newspaper they read.

Issue voting

All political parties outline their vision for the future and the policies to improve the quality of life of the electorate and their families (see extracts from the 2019 UK party manifestos on pages 63–64).

As highlighted, Brexit was the key issue in both the 2017 and 2019 general elections. There was also a great deal of focus on the public perception of then Labour leader Jeremy Corbyn. The majority of newspapers were hostile to the Labour leader and portrayed him as, among other things, a terrorist sympathiser and unpatriotic (a detailed coverage of the influence of the media follows in the next chapter).

The 2015 general election

The handling of the economy and the personality of the Labour leader, Ed Miliband, were the key campaign issues. Immigration and membership of the EU were the key policy issues for UKIP and its supporters. In a Lord Ashcroft poll carried out in May 2015, 87 per cent of UKIP voters regarded immigration as one of the three most important issues facing the country. (In the 2014 European election UKIP achieved a historic victory by winning the most votes and seats.) Two Conservative MPs switched to UKIP and the concern for David Cameron was that Conservative supporters hostile to the EU might switch to UKIP. This explains why the Conservatives included in their manifesto a promise to hold a referendum on UK membership of the EU.

An opinion poll at the time highlighted the public's perception of the party leaders. What was clear was that David Cameron was more popular than his party; in contrast the Labour Party was more popular than its leader Ed Miliband. (Around 79 per cent of Conservative voters had the competence of David Cameron as one of the three main reasons for their choice. In contrast only 39 per cent of Labour voters gave this as a reason for their choice.)

The threat from the north

Opinion polls predicted a hung parliament and the possibility of the SNP being the 'King-makers'; Conservatives played on this fear among English voters by campaigning on a negative platform that a vote for Labour would make Alex Salmond the puppet-master. Conservative election billboards used this theme (see Figure 4.3).

Figure 4.3 **Conservative billboard showing Ed Miliband in the pocket of Alex Salmond**

The 2017 and 2019 general elections

The image of the party leaders and the policies of the political parties were important factors in explaining the results of these general elections. In 2017, the Labour leader, Jeremy Corbyn, came across far better than expected to the public at large. In contrast, Theresa May, whose leadership slogan was 'strong and stable', came across as wooden and unwilling to engage with the public. She refused to participate in the television debate with other party leaders. Labour's policy on leaving the EU was to accept the referendum result but to negotiate a soft Brexit (see page 14). This enabled Labour to switch the debate to social and economic policies and the impact of austerity. In contrast, May's policy on social care for older people was referred to as the 'dementia tax'. The Conservatives made a quick U-turn to cancel the policy but the damage had been done. This undermined May's claim of being a strong and stable leader. The result was not a Conservative landslide but rather the disaster for May of a minority Tory government.

May's failure to win a comfortable overall majority weakened her power and authority. She failed three times to get her Brexit deal through parliament and lost control of the parliamentary process. The

EU gave the UK an extension and Boris Johnson replaced May as prime minister. Though he negotiated a new deal with the EU, he lost the support of the DUP; as such, he was prime minister only in name as the opposition parties controlled the parliamentary agenda. However, the opposition parties made the mistake of supporting a government proposal to end the deadlock by holding another general election.

Once again, the image of the party leaders and party policies were crucial, with the issue of Brexit central to both. It was clear that the UK population was suffering from 'Brexit fatigue' and was tired of the indecision among the political leaders. As such, the Conservative slogan of 'Get Brexit Done' and Johnson's promise that a new deal was 'oven-ready' struck a chord with many English voters. In contrast, Labour's Brexit promise (see box) dismayed and angered many Labour Brexit voters. Labour seemed to have betrayed these voters by

promising to negotiate a new deal with the EU, followed by another referendum. Critics of these moves felt that Corbyn came across as indecisive and a man not to be trusted. In contrast, despite his own patchy reputation, Johnson was regarded as the saviour of the 2016 referendum result. As such, Labour's extensive manifesto (see pages 63–64), with a promise to end austerity through massive spending, did not make the intended impact. The voters were no longer willing to give Corbyn the benefit of the doubt. In the runup to the election the Labour leader had the lowest poll numbers of any leader of the opposition since records began – his net-satisfaction rate was minus 60. Labour candidates in Labour-held seats that had supported Brexit were aware of their leader's deep unpopularity with the voters. One Labour candidate stated 'Voters did not see Mr Corbyn as a viable Prime Minister. He was nothing short of toxic' (see Table 4.8).

Labour's Brexit policies 2017 and 2019

Labour accepts the referendum result…. We will scrap the Conservative's Brexit White Paper and replace it with fresh negotiating priorities that have a strong emphasis on retaining the benefits of the Single Market and the Customs Union – which are essential for maintaining industries, jobs and businesses in Britain. Labour will always put jobs and the economy first. … We will reject 'no deal' as a viable option and, if needs be, negotiate transitional arrangements to avoid a 'cliff-edge' for the UK economy.

Extract from the 2017 General Election Labour Party Manifesto

Labour will give the people the final say on Brexit. Within three months of coming to power, a Labour government will secure a sensible deal. And within six months, we will put that deal to a public vote alongside the option to remain. A Labour government will implement whatever the people decide.

Extract from the 2019 General Election Labour Party Manifesto

The collapse of the red wall: 2019 general election

It was no accident that, shortly after the election, Boris Johnson visited Sedgefield in the north of England to thank northern voters for voting Conservative, many for the first time. Many traditional Labour seats in the north of England (Labour's red wall) had gone from Labour red to Tory blue. Sedgefield had been the seat of Labour's most successful electoral leader, Tony Blair. In 1997, Blair won by a majority of 25,000; in 2019, the Conservative candidate won by 4,500 votes. Party members engaged in door-step canvassing in the constituency stated that, while some individuals gave Brexit as their reason for rejecting Labour, the majority gave Corbyn as their reason.

Table 4.8 **What reasons did people give for not voting Labour?**

	Main reasons voters did not vote Labour in England, Scotland and Wales (%)		
	Labour's leadership	**Labour's Brexit position**	**Labour's economic policies**
Did not vote Labour (all)	43	17	12
Labour defector (all)	37	21	6
Labour defectors to Liberal Democrats	29	15	5
Labour defectors to Conservatives	45	31	6

Source: Opinium 2019

Summary of main policies of the political parties at the 2019 general election

Conservative

- To 'Get Brexit Done' in January 2020 and unleash the potential of the whole country
- To introduce an Australian-style points system to control immigration
- Not to raise the rate of income tax, VAT or national insurance
- To employ 20,000 more police and bring in tougher sentencing for criminals
- To give extra funding to the NHS, with 50,000 more nurses and 6000 more GPs a year
- To reach Net Zero by 2050 with investment in clean energy solutions and green infrastructure to reduce carbon emissions and pollution
- To invest millions in education, especially in science schools, infrastructure and apprenticeships

Adapted from 'Our Plan: Conservative Manifesto 2019'

Labour

- To increase public sector pay by 5 per cent
- To scrap Universal Credit and tuition fees
- To raise an additional £83 billion through a variety of measures including increasing income tax for those earning more than £80,000 and increasing inheritance tax and corporation tax ⇨

- To introduce free TV licences for over-75s and no dental charges for all
- To provide free full-fibre broadband and free bus travel for over-75s
- To nationalise the Royal Mail, energy, water, rail, bus networks and parts of British Telecom

- To build more council houses and bring in rent caps

Adapted from 'It's Time for Real Change: The Labour Party Manifesto 2019'

Liberal Democrats

- To stop Brexit – revoke Article 50 and cancel Brexit
- To introduce a penny income tax rise for the NHS
- To recruit 20,000 more teachers
- To legalise cannabis

- To give zero-hours workers a 20 per cent pay rise
- To build 300,000 new homes a year
- To generate 80 per cent of electricity from renewables
- To freeze train fares

Adapted from 'Stop Brexit: Build a Brighter Future', Liberal Democrats manifesto, 2019

SNP

- To demand the democratic right of the people of Scotland to decide their own future by holding a second Scottish referendum in 2020
- To keep Scotland in Europe by supporting a second Brexit referendum with the option of remaining in the EU
- To increase health spending and protect the NHS from privatisation
- To scrap Trident

- To tackle the climate emergency, with the UK government matching Holyrood climate targets
- To tackle the drug crisis, by devolving drugs classification to Scotland to enable the setting-up of consumption rooms where users could use illegal drugs
- To devolve more benefits to the Scottish Parliament and devolve employment law to protect workers' rights

Adapted from 'Stronger for Scotland – The SNP General Election Manifesto', 2019

Show your understanding

1 Outline the short-term factors that can influence elections.
2 What issues influenced voters in the 2017 general election? Explain why.
3 What issues influenced voters in the 2019 general election? Explain why.
4 Refer to Table 4.8. To what extent does it suggest that Corbyn's leadership was the most important reasons for voters not supporting Labour in England?

20-mark question

'Some factors are more important in influencing voting behaviour than others.' Discuss.

5 The influence of the media on voting behaviour

The media has four main roles to perform within society – to inform, educate, entertain and advertise. Some forms of media such as art, film and music, although often carrying a message, will be primarily produced to entertain us. Likewise, television fulfils these roles through the production of various genres of programming. For example, soaps and dramas entertain, while documentaries and the news educate and inform. Buying a newspaper or watching the television provides us with a source of information that informs and educates us about local, national and international events and, in turn, this information helps us form opinions and undoubtedly shapes our views on matters such as politics. Newspapers and news channels also have websites that many people now use instead of buying a print copy of a newspaper or watching the news on television in the evening. The development of new technology and the rise of electronic media are allowing people to access information instantly. Smartphones let people catch up with politics and current affairs in seconds by reading newspaper apps, watching the news or listening to the radio on their handset (or on a tablet). Furthermore, social media is carving an important role in the media world, with over 2 billion people accessing sites like Facebook and Twitter on a daily basis. New media developments have undoubtedly extended the UK's long history of freedom of the press and broadcasting. In short, the media has a significant and influential role to play in politics and in influencing the electorate when it comes to election time.

The media and age

You will have learned about the increasing influence of age on voting behaviour in the last chapter (see page 58). The influence of the media is also shaped by age; therefore, these two factors are inter-linked.

Recent studies indicate that younger people, aged 18–30, have largely abandoned TV news and print media altogether and mainly get their news from internet-based outlets such as websites and social media. In contrast, people over the age of 60 still tend to rely on TV bulletins and print media to get their news. Therefore, there is a clear difference in terms of media and news consumption along age lines and this is important in understanding the influence of the media on voting behaviour.

Newspapers

The newspaper industry is controlled by a small number of wealthy people who own and dominate the main publications. Over three-quarters of the press is owned by a handful of billionaires, with Rupert Murdoch and Lord Rothermere owning over half between them, including popular titles such as *The Sun*, the *Daily Mail*, *The Times* and *The Metro*. Ever since *The Sun*'s 1992 notorious front-page headline 'It's the Sun wot won it', claiming credit for the Conservatives' victory, there has been an ongoing debate among academics and political strategists about the extent to which any one paper can influence voters. Undoubtedly, however, newspapers have traditionally played a huge part in UK politics and continue to influence political parties, politicians, decision making and the electorate.

Political bias

An important aspect of newspaper publication is the fact that newspapers are allowed to be politically biased in their reporting. Therefore, the decision of a popular newspaper to show favour towards or even promote a particular party can be said to be an influence on the electorate. This is because in the UK approximately 10 per cent of the population still read a print copy of a newspaper every day, and tend to be loyal to the newspaper they read. This 10 per cent, roughly 5 million people, absorb the biased stories they read, which can influence and shape their political views. For example, 1.2 million people read *The Sun* newspaper daily, which has supported the Conservative Party in recent elections. Every day the pro-Conservative and anti-Labour agenda of the paper is influencing over a million people. Come election time, this influence may translate into votes for the Conservatives. Interestingly, in

Scotland, the *Scottish Sun* newspaper supports the SNP and the Scottish readership of the newspaper reads pro-SNP stories. Take a look at the headlines of two newspapers from the 2019 UK general election and it is clear to see the persuasive techniques used by newspapers to influence the electorate (see Figure 5.1). Three-quarters of the national daily newspapers endorsed the Conservatives in the 2019 UK general election (see Table 5.1). This includes *The Sun*, the *Daily Mail*, *The Telegraph* and the *Daily Express*.

Newspapers not only have a 'megaphone' that lets them dominate the public debate, but they effectively set the political agenda for other media types and more widely in society. With the relentless news cycle and newspapers published every day, the drip-drip effect of stories sets the broad political consensus. Newspapers are also becoming more and more popular online, with digital versions boasting roughly the same readership figures as their traditional print format. In fact, *The Guardian* has more readers online than off. This shift to digital has attracted younger readers.

Your vote has never been more vital. Today, you MUST brave the deluge to go to your local polling station and back…
BORIS

FOR THEM… The NHS, TV licences, Our schools, Child poverty, Grenfell, Crime victims, Homeless, Nurses,
VOTE LABOUR

Figure 5.1 Newspaper headlines from the *Daily Mail* (left) and the *Daily Mirror* (right) from the 2019 UK general election day

Political spin

Newspapers and their influence on the electorate is demonstrated by the fact that political parties employ specialists in media communications to make sure the press coverage of their party is as favourable as possible. These spin doctors are not only commonplace in politics today, but they are regarded as essential, especially at election time when they become key strategists in managing parties' election campaigns. During the 2019 election campaign, the Conservatives, who went on to win the election, were advised by political strategist Dominic Cummings. It was Dominic Cummings who devised the 'Get Brexit Done' slogan that resonated with many voters. Cummings subsequently worked as a key adviser to the prime minister.

The art of *spin* in politics

With a relentlessly intrusive media (especially newspapers) that focus increasingly on personality as well as policy and events, political spin has become incredibly important in twenty-first-century politics. Political spin involves controlling communication so that it shows your own political party in a favourable light. There is an obvious attraction for political parties to be able to manage news output and public relations. Media specialists, or spin doctors, can put a positive spin on negative stories and have close relationships with journalists to whom they leak certain stories. A spin doctor understands that releasing a major piece of negative news to the media, such as cuts to the police budget, should be done at a certain time or during certain circumstances. For example, there may be a significant national or global event that will most certainly be front page news on a particular day and therefore that day would be referred to as a *good day to bury bad news*. Ironically, political spinning and spin doctors in particular have a poor public reputation, as the practice of spinning stories is seen as manipulating the truth. It can be argued that spin doctors damage transparency (openness and honesty) in UK politics. Ultimately, they exist to ensure the electorate favour the party that employs them.

The declining influence of newspapers

Falling circulation

According to the Audit Bureau of Circulations (which specialises in measurement of media publication) figures show that, since January 2001, the total circulation of the UK's ten major national newspapers has declined from 12 million on average each day to a daily average of 5 million in 2020 – a decline of over 50 per cent. If the same trend continues over the following 20 years, the newspaper industry will collapse. Despite circulation falling, newspapers remain very important to politicians and political parties but perhaps decreasingly so.

Table 5.1 **Average daily newspaper circulation 2018–2020 and 2019 election bias**

Newspaper	Jan. 2018*	Jan. 2019*	Jan. 2020*	2019 election bias
The Sun	1,545,594	1,410,896	1,250,634	Conservative
Daily Mail	1,343,142	1,246,568	1,169,241	Conservative
Daily Mirror	583,192	508,705	451,466	Labour
The Times	440,558	417,298	368,929	Conservative
The Guardian	152,714	141,160	132,341	Labour
The Daily Record	134,087	119,328	104,343	Anti-Conservative

* Source: www.abc.org.uk

Tabloid political content

The most popular daily newspapers bought by the electorate are tabloid newspapers. The tabloids tend to focus more on 'soft news' such as lifestyle, entertainment and human-interest stories. Political articles only take up a few pages in a tabloid newspaper. It is likely that, for a significant number of people who buy tabloids, the main reason for their purchase is to read the sports pages, crime stories or the glossy magazine contained inside the paper. People may even be a regular buyer of a particular newspaper to read the horoscopes or to do the daily crossword. Aside from occasional front-page political news, it would be incorrect to assume that millions of people are digesting political and economic news every day from popular newspapers. Broadsheets such as *The Times* and *The Guardian* contain more complex political analysis, but these newspapers are much less popular. More people read *The Sun* on a daily basis than *The Times*, *The Observer*, *The Telegraph*, and *The Guardian* combined.

Television

As much as newspapers are often considered to be the most politically influential form of media, television is still a powerful medium of influence with the public. This is despite the fact that television must remain politically impartial.

Television has such power because it remains the major source of news consumption: in 2019, it was reported that 75 per cent of UK adults still claim to rely on television to tell them what's happening. Headline stories in TV news programmes such as the main six and ten o'clock news can put the government under intense scrutiny and highlight failures to the electorate. The same is true of analytical programmes such as *Newsnight*, *Panorama* and *Question Time*, where enormous pressure can be put on the government to account for their actions and policies. There have been many occasions when government ministers have floundered under the intense questioning of presenters such as Jeremy Paxman, Sophy Ridge and Andrew Neil. The electorate watch the news and these various programmes in their millions, and this can shape and form opinions about parties and their leaders.

TV debates and interviews

Over the last decade, television's political influence has moved beyond reporting news to including TV debates and audience-led interviews with leading politicians. Political TV debates have become a standing feature of elections and referenda in the UK since 2010. In 2010 there was a series of debates between the leaders of the 'big three' UK parties of that time (Labour, Conservative and Liberal Democrat).

However, in 2019, multiple TV debates took place between the leaders of many of the parties with representation in parliament. There were also regional TV debates and even debates on specific issues such as climate change and Brexit.

The main live televised leaders' debates of 2019 allowed the main parties to reach voters in their own homes and speak directly to them. As a result, TV debates carry a certain degree of influence. Party leaders are conscious that an ill-considered sound bite or a flustered moment live on TV can have damaging consequences for their reputation and electoral chances. The electorate at home are listening to every word, watching body language and evaluating temperament while expecting to be entertained and engaged.

In 2019, Conservative leader Boris Johnson continuously avoided TV debates; he only took part in a very small number, including a direct debate with Jeremy Corbyn. Johnson also avoided interviews with challenging presenters such as Andrew Neil. It was reported that Johnson's performance when in front of the camera in a live format was worrying for his campaign team as he seemed to come across as bumbling and arrogant. Johnson had a particularly difficult evening during a live BBC audience Q&A when he was grilled on past indiscretions and called a liar by the audience. However, the Conservatives went on to win the 2019 election comfortably and Johnson became prime minister. It is possible that, as some sections of the media suggested, Johnson's team made a tactical choice to minimise his exposure on live television during the election campaign, and it seems the appearances he made did not damage his electoral performance.

Figure 5.2 **Leaders' TV debates, 2019 UK general election**

Party election broadcasts

Party election broadcasts are 'adverts' produced by political parties to be shown on television (and increasingly on social media) in the runup to an election, with the aim of persuading people to vote for them come election day. They are often screened during prime-time television shows and are therefore guaranteed large audiences. The broadcast may only be a few minutes long but having the undivided attention of 5 million people who are glued to the television set in their living room is something many other forms of media cannot offer. The importance of the party election broadcast was underlined during the 2019 UK general election campaign, when all of the main parties produced several adverts for both television and social media. Different parties took different approaches. For example, the Conservatives took the opportunity to carefully produce stage-managed adverts for their leader, Boris Johnson, with the apparent aim of making him relatable to the public. Labour produced longer adverts for YouTube which focused on certain issues such as the NHS and inequality. Some party election broadcasts have the opposite effect to that intended, attracting negative publicity, making the party look ridiculous and putting people off voting for the party. For example, during the 2014 independence referendum campaign, Better Together produced a broadcast which was mockingly renamed 'patronising BT lady' on social media. The advert received lots of negative feedback from voters and the broadcast was quickly pulled.

Radio

Radio can be an after-thought when discussing the media's influence on the electorate but with advancements in technology such as digital radio, it is still very much a popular source of news and information for many people, especially those who are older. The *Today* programme on BBC Radio 4 is an early morning news and current affairs programme with around 7 million daily listeners at the time of writing. It provides regular news bulletins, along with serious and often confrontational political interviews and in-depth reports from BBC heavyweights such as Nick Robinson and Mishal Husain. Digital station LBC (Leading Britain's Conversation) has become increasingly popular over recent years with numerous high-profile political guests appearing on air to do interviews and phone-ins. LBC has been described as pushing the limit of the public service broadcasting requirement to be politically balanced. Unlike the BBC, it encourages its presenters, such as James O'Brien, to broadcast their views and share their personal experiences.

Show your understanding

1 With reference to newspapers, describe political bias.
2 How many people still read newspapers in the UK on a daily basis?
3 Why might *The Sun* be described as a very influential newspaper? Give reasons for your answer.
4 Explain political spin with reference to 'The art of *spin* in politics' box.
5 Explain why falling circulation is reducing the political influence of newspapers on the electorate. Make reference to the figures in Table 5.1.
6 Why might the influence of **tabloid** newspapers be overstated?
7 With reference to television, describe political impartiality.
8 'TV debates are very influential on the electorate at election time.' To what extent is this statement true?
9 Outline the influence of party election broadcasts.

Social media

The internet is now a huge part of everyone's life. Many people would find it unthinkable to go a day without going online on their phone, tablet or computer. The rise in the use and popularity of the internet over the last decade can mainly be attributed to the growth of social media sites such as Facebook, Instagram and Twitter, and sites such as YouTube. In 2021, 90 per cent of households in Great Britain had internet access, up from 73 per cent in 2010. The internet was accessed every day, or almost every day, by over 90 per cent of adults in Great Britain in 2021, compared with 35 per cent in 2006, when directly comparable records began. This is mainly due to the advancement of internet-enabled smartphones. Almost all adults aged 16–24 (96 per cent) accessed the internet 'on the go', compared with only 29 per cent of those aged 65 years and over. Social networking was used by 66 per cent of adults, and of those, 79 per cent did so every day or almost every day. Over the last decade, use of the internet has more than doubled; therefore the influence of social media on voting behaviour is worthy of consideration.

Due to its ever-increasing popularity over the last few years, social media has become the most common way for the public to connect with politicians and it is the main way that young voters consume news. The vast majority of Britain's 650 MPs are now on Twitter and are using it progressively more. In total, UK MPs sent over a million tweets last year and leading politicians such as Nicola Sturgeon have millions of followers. The level of engagement by politicians on social media has exploded in the last few years and it is now beyond doubt that social media is a critical part of how an MP/MSP communicates with the outside world. In addition, it has boosted the personal image of many MPs, who have benefited from revealing shades of personality through their Twitter messages. Tweeting in an informal way about shopping, weekend plans and hobbies reinforces their human side, boosting likeability in an era of low trust in politicians. This in turn can influence the electorate and win votes. Similarly, social media can also be used cleverly to engage voters using viral videos, gifs and memes. In 2019, Jeremy Corbyn used memes frequently to appeal to the youth vote.

Polling station: come over
Me: I can't, it's too cold outside
Polling station: Boris Johnson is going to sell off our NHS
Me:

3:05 PM · Dec 10, 2019 · Twitter Media Studio

34.6K Retweets   **4,228** Quote Tweets   **159.5K** Likes

Figure 5.3 A popular meme posted on Twitter by Jeremy Corbyn. Source: Twitter

However, a slip-up or poorly worded comment on social media can seriously damage, if not ruin, a political career. SNP MP Mhairi Black's Twitter use came back to haunt her during the 2015 general election campaign when the print media dug up old tweets from her teenage years. Black had sent some controversial tweets as a 16-year-old about drinking and football, which led to some calling for Nicola Sturgeon to deselect her as the SNP candidate for Paisley and Renfrewshire South. Similarly, in 2020 Labour's shadow education secretary, Rebecca Long-Bailey, was sacked by party leader, Sir Keir Starmer, for sharing an article on Twitter which contained an anti-Semitic conspiracy theory. Social media has also become awash with click bait and fake news that undermine democracy but can influence unwitting social media users.

Snapchat – capturing the youth vote

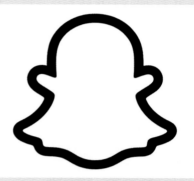

During the 2019 campaign, parties also spent some of their campaign funds on Snapchat in an attempt to influence the younger voter (around 77 per cent of 18–24-year-olds are Snapchat users, according to communications firm Cast From Clay). Facebook, whose audience has become older over time, is used less by the 18–24 demographic, who are more inclined to align with left-wing values. Labour spent five times more on Snapchat than the Conservatives, pushing adverts and even creating 'I'm voting Labour' geofilters that users could add to pictures and videos. Also, Jeremy Corbyn was the first UK party leader to have his own Snapchat profile. However, spending on Snapchat advertising was still far exceeded by spending on Instagram and Facebook.

Social media adverts

In recent years there has been a significant increase in political advertising on social media platforms such as Facebook. With an estimated 40 million users in the UK, many of whom specify their age, gender, ethnic background, where they live and their personal interests, Facebook is a gold mine of personal data. This information gives parties an unprecedented opportunity to tailor and personalise adverts to specific niches of the electorate. This is controversial in the sense that only the intended audience will see the advert. Parties pay for their ads to be viewed by a certain demographic, for example 18–24-year-olds who are at university. Another controversy of social media advertising in 2019 was the accuracy and truthfulness of some published adverts. Fact-checking of political adverts is not a legal requirement so parties may push the boundaries of their messages. Full Fact, the UK's leading fact-checking charity, found that the three main UK parties were all guilty of publishing 'misleading political adverts' on Facebook. Full Fact found the Conservatives to be the worst offenders, with 88 per cent of their Facebook adverts being labelled misleading by Full Fact. For example, 5132 Conservative ads claimed that the Conservatives would build '40 new hospitals', either in the caption, image or link. The claim was labelled as misleading by Full Fact who showed Boris Johnson's government had actually announced plans to build six hospitals, not 40. The Liberal Democrats were also criticised for including misleading graphs in their social media adverts. The furore over political ads in 2019 led to Twitter CEO Jack Dorsey banning all political advertising on the platform stating, 'political message reach should be earned, not bought'.

Figure 5.4 **Social media advert**

Nevertheless, during the 2019 general election campaign, parties spent millions on Facebook; the Conservatives spent almost £1 million in the final two weeks of the campaign alone. This highlights that parties see social media as an effective influence as they tend to spend a significantly large amount of their budget on creating these ads, which people will see while scrolling through their feeds.

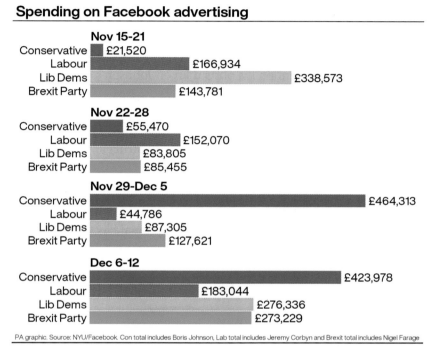

Spending on Facebook advertising

Nov 15-21
Conservative	£21,520
Labour	£166,934
Lib Dems	£338,573
Brexit Party	£143,781

Nov 22-28
Conservative	£55,470
Labour	£152,070
Lib Dems	£83,805
Brexit Party	£85,455

Nov 29-Dec 5
Conservative	£464,313
Labour	£44,786
Lib Dems	£87,305
Brexit Party	£127,621

Dec 6-12
Conservative	£423,978
Labour	£183,044
Lib Dems	£276,336
Brexit Party	£273,229

PA graphic. Source: NYU/Facebook. Con total includes Boris Johnson, Lab total includes Jeremy Corbyn and Brexit total includes Nigel Farage

Figure 5.5 Spending of the three main UK political parties on Facebook adverts in the four weeks leading up to the 2019 general election

Social media bubbles

The scale, size and popularity of social media mean it is easy to assume that it must be massively influential come election time. However, the experience of recent elections suggests this influence is not in fact as significant as many would expect. A main reason for this is the **echo-chamber effect**. As much as people who use the internet are now exposed to more views and opinions than ever before, many people end up creating a digital echo-chamber on their social media platforms. An echo-chamber is an environment in which a person encounters only beliefs or opinions that coincide with their own, so that their existing views are reinforced and alternative ideas are not considered. For example, although people on Twitter may feel they are engaging with the wider world, many often only follow people they know, agree with or respect. This means they are less likely to be exposed to, and influenced by, diversity and difference of opinion. They only experience political views on Twitter that broadly agree with their own and some in turn attack those who have opposing views. For example, if someone is already a left-wing Labour supporter then their social media platforms will likely reflect this – which in turn reduces the chances they would be influenced to vote for anyone else. See the case study on the influence of Twitter on page 75.

Social media influence in question as Labour wins the battle online but loses the election

Last Thursday's UK general election saw a disastrous defeat for the Labour Party, to the surprise of those following the campaign only on social media. The online battle for hearts and minds was a triumph for Jeremy Corbyn's Labour Party, with slick videos, memes and Facebook posts all going viral. Boris Johnson's Conservatives had much less impact on the internet, by comparison.

This impression is supported by social media metrics measuring the online campaigns of the two main competing parties. Analytics tools confirm that the Labour leader gained far more Twitter and Facebook followers than the Conservative leader throughout the election campaign. Corbyn's supporters also were more involved, with far greater engagement on his posts than on Johnson's.

Always alive to capturing the youth vote, the Labour Party capitalised on any opportunity to deliver a blow to the Conservatives on social media, particularly through 'attack videos'. These clever clips were edited by a team of cyber-activists for Momentum, a left-wing grassroots movement. Many went viral. The video of Nicky Morgan, the culture secretary of the Conservative Party, struggling with the meaning of the word 'more' in relation to the number of NHS nurses in ten years' time, attracted millions of views.

Such viral moments, often deemed at the time to have 'broken the internet', in the end didn't appear to cut through to the wider population, nor did they translate into votes.

The significance of winning the social-media war ahead of the general election had already been called into question in 2015, when the then-prime minister David Cameron won the election but lost the battle of the internet. He famously claimed at the time that 'Britain and Twitter are not the same thing'. In 2019, with a Conservative win of 364 seats to Labour's 203, his point holds true.

ICT task

In groups of three, create a PowerPoint to be presented to the class on the influence of social media political advertising. Make reference to various social media platforms and parties, spending totals and the 2019 general election. Come to an overall conclusion on how influential these adverts are in terms of voting behaviour.

Case study: The influence of Twitter – a force for good in politics?

Social media platforms, such as Twitter, Facebook and YouTube, provide ways to stimulate citizen engagement in political life and drive up what is known as e-participation and social media activism. Personal communication via social media brings politicians and parties closer to their potential voters. It allows politicians to communicate faster and reach citizens in a more targeted manner and vice versa, without the intermediate role of mass media. Twitter in particular has been responsible for a boom in e-participation. Reactions, feedback, conversations and debates about political events are generated online, as well as support for and participation in offline events (see pressure groups in Chapter 8, page 126). Through Twitter's hashtagging feature, political movements and gestures have gathered momentum through 'trending' and have entered mainstream politics. During the 2015 UK election campaign, Twitter was a source of joy for Ed Miliband when a 17-year-old social media activist managed to get huge support for him via her #Milifandom hashtag. According to the hashtag creator, Milifandom aimed to generate online support for Miliband as he was being 'bullied by Rupert Murdoch's newspapers'. Milifandom entered mainstream society and was regularly used by Miliband as a way of improving his often-derided image.

However, Twitter's increasing role in politics has been criticised by many. As with all social media platforms, Twitter allows a degree of anonymity and people tend to say things on Twitter they would not say in person. Although Twitter may be responsible for a rise in participation, much of this participation is negative. Many politicians receive daily personal abuse and some even received death threats via Twitter during the 2019 election campaign. Social media has given a new platform for politics and political activism for people in the UK, as it has done with sport, showbiz and news.

Show your understanding

1 a) Outline statistics to show the rise of internet and social media use.
   b) Provide evidence to show the significant increase in social media use by politicians.
2 a) How can politicians use social media to influence voters?
   b) Why do politicians need to be careful with their use of social media?
3 Why is Facebook an attractive platform for political advertising?
4 Why is social media advertising controversial? Explain, in detail, with examples.
5 Outline party spending on Facebook in the lead up to the 2019 UK general election.
6 Explain the echo-chamber effect and why it suggests social media has limited influence on voters.
7 Using the newspaper article on page 74, explain why social media influence appears limited.
8 Read the Twitter case study above. Have a class discussion on whether Twitter is a good or bad influence on politics in the UK. Write a summary of your views.

12-mark question

Analyse the influence of the media on voting behaviour.

Representative democracy in Scotland

6

Background

Almost 300 years since the Act of Union dissolved the Scottish Parliament, a referendum was held on proposals for a directly elected Scottish Parliament with wide legislative powers. On 11 September 1997, these proposals received overwhelming support from the people of Scotland. The turnout was 60.4 per cent, with 74.3 per cent voting in favour of a Scottish Parliament and 60.2 per cent for the parliament to have tax-varying powers. This result was enough for Prime Minister Tony Blair to say, 'This is a good day for Scotland, and a good day for Britain and the United Kingdom … the era of big centralised government is over.' The following year, the Scotland Act (1998) cleared a pathway for the creation once again of a Scottish Parliament with the power to pass laws affecting Scotland in a variety of areas, known as devolved matters, which have been extended over the years (see page 8).

Figure 6.1 **The Scottish Parliament**

Devolution

Devolution is the transfer or delegation of powers to a lower level, especially by central government to a local or regional administration. In the UK, some powers have been transferred from the UK Parliament at Westminster to various nations and regions. For example, different powers have been devolved to the Scottish Parliament, the National Assembly for Wales and the Northern Ireland Assembly. There are also levels of devolution in London and northern cities such as Manchester, which has control over its own health budget as well as having its own mayor. The UK now has three Executives, with devolved powers for 16.4 per cent of the population and one government for England and the UK. (See Chapters 1 and 2 for a full overview of constitutional arrangements.)

The functions of the Scottish Parliament

The Scottish Parliament has four founding principles, which aim to create an effective and accountable parliament, answering the needs of the people of Scotland. The four principles are: sharing power, accountability, openness and participation, and equal opportunities. In achieving the four founding principles, the Scottish Parliament regards itself as a model of modern democracy. For example, the Scottish Parliament should embody and reflect the sharing of power between the people of Scotland, the legislators and the Scottish government.

Furthermore, the Scottish Parliament should be accessible, open and responsive; it should develop procedures that make possible a participative approach to the development, consideration and scrutiny of policy and legislation.

The difference between the Scottish Parliament and the Scottish government

The Scottish Parliament comprises all 129 elected Members of the Scottish Parliament (MSPs) and is the law-making body for devolved matters. It considers proposed legislation and scrutinises the activities and policies of the Scottish government through debates, parliamentary questions and the work of committees. The Scottish government (or Scottish Executive) is the government in Scotland for devolved matters and, as such, it is responsible for defining and implementing policy in these areas. It is headed by the first minister and is made up of those MSPs who have been appointed by the first minister as cabinet secretaries and ministers.

The Scottish Executive

The Scottish government (legally referred to as the Scottish Executive) is the government in Scotland in charge of devolved matters. The Scottish Executive is responsible for formulating and implementing policy in these areas and is led by the first minister, who is nominated by the Scottish Parliament and appointed by the monarch. They in turn appoint Scottish ministers to make up a cabinet but only with the agreement of parliament and the approval of the monarch. Cabinet members are referred to as cabinet secretaries.

The role of the first minister and the Executive

The first minister is the head of the devolved Scottish government. They lead the Scottish cabinet and are responsible for the development, implementation and presentation of government policy, constitutional affairs, and promoting and representing Scotland. The first minister is also directly accountable to the Scottish Parliament for their actions and the actions of the Scottish government. There is no fixed term of office for the first minister and, after appointment, the first minister can remain in position until they resign, are dismissed or die. There have been five first ministers in the short history of the Scottish Parliament since 1999: the first, Donald Dewar, died in office and the second, Henry McLeish, resigned. In both of these circumstances, it was the responsibility of the presiding officer to appoint someone to serve as first minister in the interim, until the Scottish Parliament decided on a new nominee to be presented to the monarch for formal appointment. The third, Jack McConnell, left office after the 2007 election, which saw the SNP become the biggest party in the parliament, with Alex Salmond named as first minister. When Alex Salmond resigned after the 2014 referendum result, Nicola Sturgeon became first minister. Sturgeon remains in post following the SNP's victory in the last election.

The term 'Scottish ministers' collectively refers to the first minister, the cabinet secretaries, the lord advocate and the solicitor general, who together make up the Scottish government. Each cabinet secretary is responsible for a particular department and indicates to the parliament what actions their department intends to take, and what legislation it wants the parliament to agree to. The government is accountable to the parliament for its actions. In the 2011–16 Scottish Parliament, the SNP held a majority of seats: 69 out of 129. This allowed the SNP to push on with implementing their policies as they could rely on majority support in parliament. However, as with 2016, following the 2021 election, the SNP no longer hold a majority of the seats (64 out of 129). This means that the SNP government have to work with other parties to pass legislation. The SNP's 2014 referendum was only achievable due to their 2011 majority. Furthermore, the lord advocate (the chief legal officer of the Scottish government) and the solicitor general are members of the Scottish Executive, as set out in the Scotland Act (1998). However, after becoming first minister, Alex Salmond decided that the lord advocate should no longer attend the Scottish cabinet stating that he wished to 'de-politicise the post'. The role of the lord advocate could further change following the 2021 Holyrood inquiry into how First Minister Nicola Sturgeon and others handled harassment claims made against Alex Salmond.

The role of the first minister

The first minister has the power to appoint MSPs to become cabinet secretaries and ministers, who form the Executive. They also have the power to reshuffle the cabinet and replace any secretaries who they feel are under-performing. The first minister sets the agenda and chairs cabinet meetings and is primarily responsible for the formulation and introduction of Scottish government policy. The first minister is also the face of the Scottish government and represents Scotland in devolved matters as well as representing Scotland abroad when building foreign relations. The first minister is accountable to the Scottish Parliament, which keeps their powers in check. The first minister faces questions every Thursday in First Minister's Questions (FMQs) when opposition leaders scrutinise the government's work (see page 89).

Figure 6.2 First Minister Nicola Sturgeon

The Scottish government is responsible for devolved matters, most of which affect the day-to-day lives of the people of Scotland, for example, health, education, justice, rural affairs and transport. It manages an annual budget of around £50 billion and each cabinet secretary is responsible for a particular department. Ministers are therefore part of two separate organisations: the Scottish Executive (as cabinet secretaries or ministers) and the Scottish Parliament (as MSPs). In addition to a constituency or regional office dealing with local matters, they may also have a ministerial office within a Scottish Executive building, dealing with ministerial responsibilities. The term 'Scottish government' is also used as a collective term to describe Scottish ministers, including civil servants. The Scottish government and the Scottish Parliament are accountable to the people of Scotland.

The Scottish cabinet

The Scottish cabinet usually meets on a weekly basis, but only while parliament is sitting. It consists of the first minister and other Scottish ministers (cabinet secretaries), excluding the Scottish law officers (the lord advocate and the solicitor general). The lord advocate attends meetings of the cabinet only when requested by the first minister.

The Scottish government operates on the basis of collective responsibility. This means that all decisions reached by ministers, individually or collectively, are binding for all members of the government. Collective responsibility does not mean that ministers must all agree on decisions; instead, membership of the government requires them to maintain a united front once decisions have been made. The Scottish government consists of 10 cabinet secretaries (including the first minister), 12 ministers and 2 law officers.

Figure 6.3 **The Scottish cabinet, 2021**

The civil service

The civil service in Scotland is part of the wider UK home civil service as it is a matter reserved by the UK Parliament and not a matter devolved to the Scottish Parliament. While the permanent secretary of the Scottish civil service, Leslie Evans, is the most senior civil servant in Scotland and heads the strategic board of the Scottish Executive, she remains answerable to the most senior civil servant in the UK, the cabinet secretary. However, those civil servants who work for the Scottish government primarily serve the devolved administration rather than the UK government.

Potential conflict

The Civil Service Code (Scottish Executive version) states that civil servants in Scotland are 'accountable to Scottish ministers who are, in turn, accountable to the Scottish Parliament', and it advises that they are at the same time 'an integral and key part of the government of the United Kingdom'. This is a compromising situation and some argue that civil servants working for the Scottish government owe their loyalty to the devolved administration rather than to the UK government. Currently, civil servants in Scotland are working directly for an SNP administration and their colleagues in London are working directly for a Conservative administration. This sounds problematic but the civil service has to remain politically neutral and unbiased on issues such as independence.

Nevertheless, the core problem is that in reality the civil service is serving two governments of different political ideologies at the same time. Therefore, a situation of conflict could develop when a civil servant serving a Conservative minister in Westminster has to talk to or brief a civil servant in Edinburgh who serves an SNP minister. If the matter is a confidential one, the exchange of details may be limited because they both know that the information will be shared with the opposing ministers.

The Sewel Convention

A Legislative Consent Motion (formerly a Sewel Motion) is when, in certain circumstances, the Scottish Parliament may give its consent for Westminster to legislate for Scotland on devolved matters. Some government policies on reserved matters can have significant implications for Scotland through their potential impact on the policies of the Scottish government, who will have to implement them in Scotland. Generally speaking, however, Legislative Consent Motions work in favour of the Scottish Parliament as they are only used when it would be more effective to legislate on a UK basis in order to put in place a single UK-wide ruling. Furthermore, a Legislative Consent Motion ensures that Westminster will normally legislate on devolved matters only with the express agreement of the Scottish Parliament, after proper consideration and scrutiny of the proposal in question. To facilitate that scrutiny, the UK government advises the Scottish Parliament as early as possible of any bill that is likely to be subject to a Legislative Consent Motion and will provide the relevant committee with a detailed memorandum explaining the purpose and effect of any devolved provisions as soon as possible after it is introduced. The committee will then be able to consider the proposal, taking evidence from interested parties if it considers that necessary, before making a recommendation to the full parliament as to whether it should approve the Legislative Consent Motion. The Scottish Parliament is free to withhold consent and reject a motion. However, it could be argued that this set-up highlights that Westminster is still the more powerful partner in the arrangement.

Financing the Scottish government

One of the most controversial questions facing politicians on both sides of the border is how the Scottish government is financed. Differences of opinion on this issue can threaten good relations between Scotland and the rest of the UK. It is not a new question insofar as it has long been claimed that Scotland received more than its fair share of British public expenditure in the pre-devolution era. Such 'discrepancies' are partly based on different levels of deprivation across British regions. Part of the explanation for Scotland's apparently favoured and privileged position lies in its relatively large territorial size and low population density outside the central belt, which means that expenditure per person for the same level of services such as education and healthcare is higher (Scotland's population is 8 per cent of the UK's).

With an SNP administration in Holyrood and a Conservative government in Westminster, there is an intensification of the controversy along national lines, with some representatives of English regions renewing their complaint that they are unfairly treated. This has been countered by Scottish claims that these differentials are justifiable on the grounds of need and Scotland's contribution to the British Treasury from North Sea oil revenues. The dilemma for any English politicians looking for a reduction in Scottish public expenditure is that cutting Scotland's budget might strengthen the SNP's case for independence referendum number two.

The Barnett formula

Essentially the Barnett formula means that, for every £1 the UK government distributes, 85p goes to England, 10p to Scotland and 5p to Wales. With a population of 5 million people, Scotland has only around 8 per cent of the UK population but gets a fixed quota of 10 per cent of the cash for public services. This has led to a situation where spending in Scotland on public services is £2,000 higher per person than in England.

Relations with Westminster

Since 2007 and the SNP's rise to a position of considerable power, relations between the Scottish government and Westminster have been increasingly strained. Under the SNP, Scotland held the 2014 independence referendum, which almost put an end to the UK as we know it. Currently, the SNP holds power, enjoys huge support in Scotland and still has independence as their principal aim. The UK has a Conservative government that is further to the right politically than the SNP. Added to this, the result of the 2019 UK general election sent 48 SNP MPs to Westminster who continue to oppose Conservative policy on a daily basis. In comparison, the Conservatives returned only six MPs.

Conflict with Westminster

COVID-19 pandemic

Throughout the COVID-19 pandemic, the devolved governments of the United Kingdom had to work together with Westminster on what was termed the 'four nations approach'. This collegiate approach meant that governments that opposed each other politically had to work together for the greater health benefit of the population. There were occasions when Scottish First Minister Nicola Sturgeon disagreed with

Prime Minister Boris Johnson but ultimately politics were put to one side in dealing with this unique issue.

Trident

In 2016, the UK government voted to renew Trident, the country's nuclear submarine system, while the Scottish Parliament voted against renewing it. Although Trident is based in Scotland, the issue of renewing Britain's nuclear deterrent is reserved by Westminster and as far as the UK government is concerned the decision has been made.

Relations with local government

In Scotland there are 32 local authorities (often referred to as councils). Some of these councils are based on county borders and cover a large geographical area while others, for example, Edinburgh and Glasgow, are based on city boundaries. These local councils have a key role in communities and impact on the daily lives of all Scottish citizens. They provide vital public services, including schools for children and care for older people; they also maintain roads, collect refuse and provide facilities for leisure and recreation. The range of services provided by the councils is extensive and the money to pay for them comes from a combination of council tax and grants from the Scottish Parliament, which in turn gets its money from the UK government. Councils spend around £20 billion each year, employ around 250,000 staff and use assets worth about £32 billion.

There are three levels of government in Scotland: the Westminster government, the Scottish Parliament and local government. Local government is the democratically elected part of government in Scotland at the local level and has an interdependent relationship with the Scottish government. The Scottish government needs local government to provide services in accordance with their priorities; in return, local authorities expect the Scottish government to provide the necessary financial resources to do so efficiently while maintaining a degree of political autonomy in order to adequately represent their local communities.

Show your understanding

1 Outline the various positions that make up the Scottish government.
2 Describe the role of the first minister.
3 What is meant by collective responsibility?
4 a) What is the role of the civil service?
   b) Why might there be conflict within the civil service?
5 Explain the Sewel Convention.
6 Describe in detail how the Scottish government is financed. Refer to the Barnett formula.
7 Since the SNP's rise to power, why have relations between the Scottish government and Westminster worsened?
8 Describe a point of conflict between the Scottish government and Westminster.
9 Outline the role of local government.
10 Describe the interdependent relationship between the Scottish government and local government.

The legislative process

A major role of any parliament is to make laws. The Scottish Parliament, in line with its founding principles, involves the whole people of Scotland along with regional and interested organisations, pressure groups and individuals, ensuring a high degree of accessibility and openness. This allows for a level of participation and the sharing of power that helps avoid a situation where the government can dominate the legislative process completely. Instead, provision is made for individual MSPs and committees to introduce or propose legislation as well as the Executive. This is important in a unicameral parliament (one with a single legislative chamber) like the Scottish Parliament.

Before they become Acts of the Scottish Parliament, legislative proposals are known as **bills**. A bill becomes an Act by being passed by the parliament and receiving royal assent.

Pre-legislative consultation

Before any legislative proposal becomes a bill it goes through a pre-legislative consultation process. This whole process is designed to allow for maximum participation in an open and accessible manner. For example, with a government bill the relevant minister informs the relevant committee of the proposed legislation and recommends which relevant groups or individuals should be involved in the pre-legislative consultation process. The Executive then consults the relevant bodies, identifying any issues of concern. The relevant committee is kept informed throughout. When the process is completed and the draft bill is introduced, the outcome of the consultation process is attached to it as a memorandum, ensuring openness from the start.

Types of bills

There are two different types of bill that can be introduced: a public bill and a private bill. All public bills are introduced by MSPs in the parliament. They may be introduced by members of the Scottish government as a government bill, by one of the parliament's committees as a committee bill or by an individual MSP as a members' bill. A private bill can be introduced by an individual or group of people.

Government bills

Introduced by a Scottish government cabinet secretary or minister, government bills account for most of the legislation passed by the Scottish Parliament. Examples of government bills include the Human Trafficking and Exploitation (Scotland) Act and the Air Weapons and Licensing (Scotland) Act.

Government bill: Age of Criminal Responsibility (Scotland) Act 2019

Introduced by: John Swinney MSP

Purpose and objectives of the bill: The intention of this bill was to raise the age of criminal responsibility from 8 to 12 years old.

Passage of the bill

The Age of Criminal Responsibility (Scotland) Act 2019 was introduced in Parliament on 13 March 2018. The Equalities and Human Rights Committee was designated as the lead committee on the bill and the Delegated Powers and Law Reform Committee was also involved. The Equalities and Human Rights Committee took stage 1 oral evidence on the general principles of the bill on 6 September 2018 and after several other meetings produced their first stage report. At stage 2, amendments were discussed in both the committee and the chamber, before amendments were then agreed upon through voting. A final debate and vote on the bill took place on 7 May 2019. The bill was passed unanimously and then received royal assent on 11 June 2019.

Source: www.parliament.scot

Committee bills

A committee bill is a public bill introduced by the **convener** of a committee of the Scottish Parliament to carry out a proposal made by the committee for a bill in relation to matters within its remit. The proposal is made by way of a report to the parliament. The bill cannot be introduced if the Scottish government or the UK government has indicated that they are planning to introduce legislation to give effect to the proposal. Between 2016 and 2021, three committee bills were introduced.

A committee convener is an MSP who chairs committee meetings. Conveners facilitate debate and, where possible, allow the committee to reach a consensus view, while acknowledging that there will be differences in the views of members.

When the first committee bill was passed by the parliament in 2001, Alasdair Morgan MSP, then convener of the Justice Committee, said: 'The ability of Scottish Parliament committees to initiate legislation is an important part of what makes our system of governance innovative and fundamentally different from Westminster.'

Members' bills

Individual MSPs, who are not members of the Scottish government, can also introduce public bills. These are termed 'members' bills'. Each MSP can introduce a maximum of two members' bills in a session. An MSP introducing a member's bill must first lodge a draft proposal giving the short title of the proposed bill and an explanation of its purpose. A member's bill must receive support from at least 18 MSPs representing at least half of the political parties (or groups) with five or more members in the parliament. (See page 92 for an example of a successful member's bill.)

Private bills

Private bills differ slightly from public bills and are subject to different procedures. A private bill is introduced by what is known as a promoter. A promoter can be an individual person, a group of people or a company; therefore, these are sometimes known as 'personal bills'. Generally, they relate to development projects or changes to the use of land and not changes to national laws.

The most well-known private bill was the Glasgow Airport Rail Link Bill, which was passed in 2007 and gave powers to the Strathclyde Passenger Transport Executive to construct a new railway service between Glasgow Airport and Glasgow Central Station. Unfortunately, the SNP government cancelled the project as a result of the recession caused by the 2008 financial crisis.

Table 6.1 **Summary of legislation, parliamentary session 5 (2016–21)**

Legislation	Government	Member's	Private	Committee	Total
Bills in progress	0	0	0	0	**0**
Bills awaiting Royal Assent	2	1	0	0	**3**
Acts of the Scottish Parliament	60	7	5	3	**75**
Bills withdrawn	1	1	0	0	**2**
Bills fallen	0	7	0	0	**7**
Total	**63**	**16**	**5**	**3**	**87**

Source: www.parliament.scot

The stages and passage of a bill

Bills need to complete three stages to become an Act of the Scottish Parliament. Committees are heavily involved from the beginning of the legislative process through to scrutinising (examining closely) proposed legislation (see pages 96–100 for more detail on the work of committees).

Stage 1: general principles (committee)

The bill is referred to the committee with the relevant subject remit, known as the lead committee. Other committees can also consider and report their views to the lead committee. In addition, the lead committee must take account of any views submitted to it by the Finance Committee. The lead committee will make recommendations about whether parliament should agree to the bill's general principles. Parliament then votes on the general principles.

Stage 2: detailed consideration (committee)

If parliament agrees to the general principles of the bill at stage 1, it then proceeds to stage 2. Here it will receive more detailed, line-by-line scrutiny by the lead committee. The committee will also consider any proposed amendments put forward by MSPs and will decide which amendments to accept. At this stage, the committee can also take further evidence. (See pages 96–100 for more detail.)

Stage 3: further detailed consideration (parliament)

If the bill proceeds to stage 3, the whole parliament will then consider and vote on whether to pass it in its amended and final form. If parliament passes the bill it goes forward for royal assent, and then becomes an Act of the Scottish Parliament.

Minority governance and the passage of legislation

The SNP govern Scotland as a minority government. This means the SNP have to compromise with other parties so they do not block legislation at every turn. This outcome empowers the Scottish Parliament, making it more like an actual legislature where compromise is at the heart of policy making. Minority government also ensures a more co-operative approach to policy making, meaning that different views and ideas are shared and more voices are heard. For example, the Scottish Greens hope to promote environmental and ecological issues during relevant policy formation. Research shows that ideology, policy preferences, electoral incentives and even personality factors can influence the behaviour of politicians. In an ideological sense, the SNP is fortunate to have parties both to its left and to its right, making it easier to get bills passed. As the SNP have 64 out of 129 seats, they only require the support of 1 MSP, presuming their own MSPs vote with their party. In the current sitting of parliament, the Greens have tended to support the SNP without being a full coalition partner.

Legislation and the UK Supreme Court

After a bill is passed by the Scottish Parliament a period of four weeks must elapse before the presiding officer can submit it for royal assent. During this period, the bill may be referred to the UK Supreme Court by the Advocate General for Scotland, the lord advocate or the attorney general on the grounds of legislative competence. The secretary of state may also block legislation under section 35 of the Scotland Act 1998 (on various grounds, including defence and national security). The bill may, however, be submitted for royal assent after less than four weeks if all three law officers and the secretary of state notify the presiding officer that they do not intend to exercise their powers under those sections.

Royal assent

The monarch must give their consent for a bill to become a law. It is a final check in a constitutional monarchy that parliament is doing a proper job in passing laws that will be suitable for the country. Nowadays it is considered a formality, as the monarch very rarely withholds royal assent.

Show your understanding

1. What is pre-legislative consultation?
2. Create a spider diagram showing the various types of bills that can be introduced in the Scottish Parliament.
3. Explain the three stages of the passing of a bill.
4. What role does the UK Supreme Court play with regards to Scottish parliamentary legislation?
5. What is royal assent?

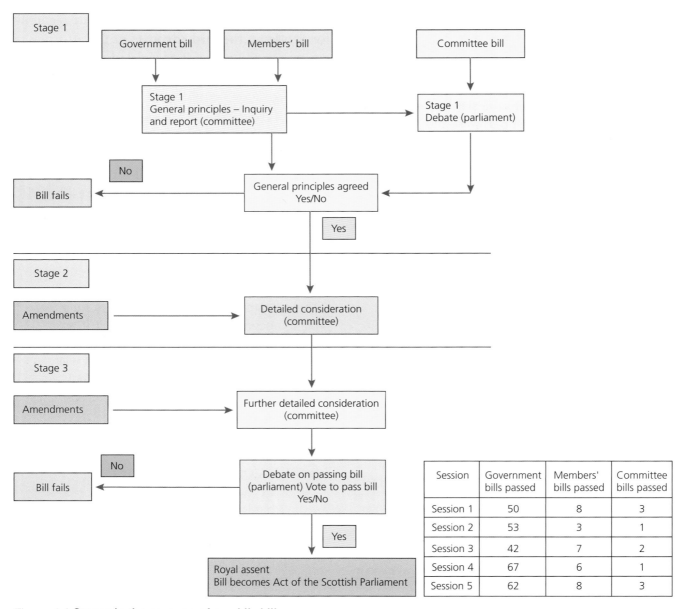

Figure 6.4 **Stages in the passage of a public bill**

Source: www.parliament.scot

The role of political representatives

The first elections for the Scottish Parliament were held on 6 May 1999, when 129 new MSPs were elected to represent and serve the people of Scotland. MSPs make decisions that shape the country and work to better the lives of their constituents. Each of the 129 MSPs represent a particular area of the country, known as a constituency or a region. There are 73 MSPs that each represent a constituency and 56 that represent 8 regions of Scotland (7 MSPs in each region).

Representation

A record 58 women MSPs (45 per cent) were elected to the sixth session of the Scottish Parliament. The previous highest proportion of female MSPs was in 2003, when the figure was 51 (40 per cent). The increase can be attributed to the efforts of political parties to improve gender balance.

In the case of the SNP, 47 per cent of their candidates were women, an increase that reflects the party's use of gender quotas in the form of all-women shortlists (AWS) in constituencies with retiring or standing down SNP MSPs. The Green Party led the way with 49 per cent of their candidates being women. In terms of Scottish Labour, the party's use of gender quotas on the list – in the form of 'zipping', or alternating, male and female candidates – meant that 10 of their 22 MSPs elected were female. Yet while the SNP and Labour's use of quotas has made a difference, the overall figures were short of equal gender representation due in large part to a strong Tory performance across Scotland. Only around 30 per cent of Scottish Conservative candidates were women.

In terms of ethnicity, progress was made at the 2021 election. In a historic moment for the Scottish Parliament, two women of colour were elected. Kaukab Stewart MSP was elected to represent the Glasgow Kelvin constituency, and Pam Gosal MSP was returned for the West of Scotland region. Pam Duncan-Glancy was also elected on the Glasgow regional list, and is the first wheelchair user to be elected to the Scottish Parliament.

Table 6.2 **Female MSPs by political party, session 6, Scottish Parliament**

Party	Constituency	Regional	Total
Conservatives	1	7	**8**
Green	0	5	**5**
Labour	1	9	**10**
Liberal Democrats	1	0	**1**
SNP	32	2	**34**
Total	**35**	**23**	**58**

Source: © Parliamentary copyright. Scottish Parliament Corporate Body

Table 6.3 **Gender representation 1999–2021**

Election	Number of female MSPs
1999	48
2003	51
2007	43
2011	45
2016	45
2021	58

Source: © Parliamentary copyright. Scottish Parliament Corporate Body

The work of an MSP and scrutiny of the Executive

The basic role of an MSP does not significantly differ from that of an MP. They primarily serve their constituents but must also work within their political party. MSPs perform work both inside and outside of parliament.

The work of an MSP inside parliament

- MSPs ask government ministers questions on behalf of their constituents or other interests. These can be written questions and/or questions posed in the Scottish Parliament (see 'Parliamentary questions').
- Much of an MSP's time in the chamber is spent debating the key issues affecting the country and on legislation that may be passing through parliament.
- As a member of a committee, MSPs have a number of duties to carry out, including scrutinising legislation and conducting inquiries.

- MSPs also have the power to attempt to introduce new bills (draft laws). They are allowed to attempt to introduce two new bills during one parliamentary session.
- MSPs vote on legislation during Decision Time. All MSPs have one vote each and so at this time all MSPs, in theory, have equal power.

The work of an MSP outside parliament

- MSPs often meet with a wide variety of people in their local constituencies. Councillors, local organisations and local pressure groups all look to meet with MSPs, hoping that any issues they have could possibly be raised at the highest levels of government.
- MSPs are expected to spend some of their time attending various events in their constituency – for example, the opening of a new business or an awards ceremony.
- In order to keep a good profile within their constituency, MSPs often appear in local newspapers or on local television and radio. Social media is also a very important form of communication (see pages 70–72).
- MSPs hold a weekly surgery so constituents can come and seek advice or make a complaint or suggestion about a local or national issue.

Parliamentary questions

Parliamentary questions are one of the key ways in which individual MSPs can **hold the government to account** and extract information relating to policies and decisions. There are various different ways in which MSPs can ask questions in the Scottish Parliament.

First Minister's Questions

Figure 6.5 **First Minister's Questions**

Every Thursday, for up to 45 minutes, MSPs can ask questions of the first minister in the chamber. Opposition leaders ask questions which are then followed by questions from backbench MSPs.

Questions from opposition leaders are not submitted beforehand and are therefore unseen by the first minister. Opposition leaders aim to ask difficult and demanding questions of the first minister which scrutinise the performance of their administration. Tough, rigorous questioning may highlight government failings and weaknesses. For example, after the 2017 publication of the Scottish Survey of Literacy and Numeracy highlighted a drop in attainment in Scottish schools, opposition leaders forced Nicola Sturgeon into admitting numeracy results were 'unacceptable'. This admission made the evening news and was in every newspaper the following day, putting the government under intense pressure and shining the spotlight on the government's education policy. Similar happened during the COVID-19 pandemic in 2021, when Nicola Sturgeon was asked weekly about her government's response to the crisis. Sturgeon faced particularly difficult questions about her response to the crisis in Scottish care homes, where death rates were extremely high, overtaking fatalities in hospitals.

However, there are some limits to the scrutiny aspect of First Minister's Questions (FMQs). The first minister has the advantage that they know some of the questions that will be asked beforehand and so can prepare answers in advance. Furthermore, the government's own backbench MSPs will ask 'friendly' questions that give the first minister the chance to outline government successes or achievements. Scrutiny is further limited due to the length of FMQs. Although the relatively recent increase from 30 minutes to 45 minutes is an improvement, 45 minutes is still a short space of time in which to hold the first minister to account, especially as some answers can be long winded. The number of questions asked of the first minister is therefore relatively small, which can be said to detract from the scrutiny aspect of the process.

Other questions

Parliament also gets the opportunity to question ministers and cabinet secretaries during General Question Time, Topical Question Time and Portfolio Question Time, although the timing for these are even shorter than the 45 minutes allocated to FMQs. At these sessions, MSPs can **hold the government to account** on specific issues such as health, justice and education.

As well as asking oral questions, MSPs can submit written questions. This format goes largely unseen and is less high profile than the event that is FMQs. However, MSPs are constantly asking written questions and they enable MSPs to ask cabinet secretaries and ministers for detailed information on any devolved matter at any time. Cabinet secretaries and ministers must reply within ten days to a submitted question. This is a very important way in which the Scottish Parliament holds the Scottish government to account. Answers are posted on the Scottish Parliament website for the public to read. See the two examples on the next page.

Written question example one

MSP: Neil Findlay, Scottish Labour

Date lodged: 16 January 2020

Written question: To ask the Scottish government what the average class size has been in (a) P1 to P3, (b) P4 to P7, (c) S1 to S3 and (d) S4 to S6 in each of the last 10 years.

Answered by John Swinney, Cabinet Secretary for Education and Skills: The Scottish government does not collect information on class sizes in the secondary sector. Information on average class sizes for P1–P3 and P4–P7 is presented in Table 1.

Table 1 Average class size for P1–P3 pupils and P4–P7 pupils, 2010–2019

Year	P1–P3	P4–P7
2010	23.2	25.9
2011	22.5	25.3
2012	22.6	25.2
2013	23.2	25.5
2014	23.3	25.7
2015	23.3	25.8
2016	23.3	26.0
2017	23.2	26.0
2018	23.2	25.9
2019	23.2	25.9

Data refers to the average class size of pupils in each stage, not the average class size of single stage classes.

Source: www.parliament.scot

Written question example two

MSP: Monica Lennon, Scottish Labour

Date lodged: 4 May 2020

Written question: To ask the Scottish government how it is ensuring the provision of free period products to people in (a) school, college and university and (b) community settings during the COVID-19 pandemic.

Answered by Aileen Campbell, Cabinet Secretary for Communities and Local Government: The Scottish government is continuing to fund access to free period products during the COVID-19 pandemic.

Local authority policy leads for both education and community provision are making reasonable adjustments to ensure products can continue to be accessed by those most in need. In wider community settings products have been redistributed to, for example, places that remain open, including community hubs. For school pupils products were made available to take home in the last few days of school, in some places there is provision of products in food boxes, and products continue to be accessible via those schools that remain open. Some local authorities have put in place home delivery options via Hey Girls and in one area products can be collected for free from a number of local convenience stores.

For college and university students, the Scottish Funding Council has liaised with Hey Girls to offer home delivery kits and redeemable online codes and a number of institutions have taken this up. Those that do not wish to take up this offer have been asked to consider alternative arrangements, but students can of course also access free products via their local community hubs.

FareShare continue to provide period products to a significant number of community groups across the country.

Source: www.parliament.scot

ICT task

In groups of three, create a PowerPoint presentation investigating the role of MSPs in scrutinising the work of the Scottish government. You will also need to refer to the section on committees (pages 94–99).

Motions

MSPs are free to propose motions for debate in parliament. Motions can also be used to highlight local issues and achievements, and to propose a course of action. Other MSPs can sign up in support of motions that have been lodged. MSPs also lodge amendments to motions to allow alternative points of view to be discussed and debated. Motions can therefore be used to express the democratic will of the parliament and can be very effective in **holding the government to account**, although in practice they do not bind the government to any action. In 2018, a Conservative motion calling for Primary 1 tests for four- and five-year-olds to be stopped was narrowly voted through by 63 to 61 (see below). This defeat for the SNP then received wide media coverage and consequently the SNP ordered a review into the impact of the tests. For motions to be as successful as this all other parties have to be united in their view against the government. Also, motions are only effective it there is a minority government in power. If the SNP enjoyed a majority, as in 2011–16, then it would be rare for a motion on government policy to result in a defeat.

Example of a motion

MSP: Liz Smith, Scottish Conservative and Unionist Party

Date lodged: 17 September 2018

Motion: Primary 1 Tests

That the parliament believes that good-quality pupil assessment is an essential component of the drive to raise educational standards in Scotland's schools, but notes the level of concern that has been raised by teachers and other education professionals regarding the introduction and delivery of new testing arrangements for Primary 1 (P1) pupils; considers that this concern questions whether the new P1 tests are in line with the play-based learning philosophy of early years provision in the curriculum for excellence, and, in light of this concern, calls on the Scottish government to halt the tests in P1 and to reconsider the evidence and the whole approach to evaluating the progress of P1 pupils.

Source: www.parliament.scot

MSPs and the party whip system

When an MSP votes in the Scottish Parliament chamber, they almost always vote the same way as their party. An MSP known as the party whip makes sure this happens and that MSPs vote along 'party lines' when backing new legislation, motions and amendments. If an MSP defies the party whip, that MSP is rebelling against their party's wishes. This happens less frequently in Scottish politics than in UK politics (see page 93).

Members' bills

MSPs are allowed to introduce two members' bills in each parliamentary session in an attempt to introduce legislation. Although members' bills will benefit wider society, many of these bills are initiated through an MSP having a personal passion for change surrounding a particular issue or topic. Only a handful of members' bills will pass each session due to the difficult process of achieving cross-party support (see page 83 for more details on bills). In rare cases, a member's bill may be very effective in **holding the government to account**. This was the case with James Kelly's (Scottish Labour) member's bill in 2018, which repealed a major government policy (see the newspaper article below).

Offensive Behaviour at Football Act abolished after member's bill is backed in Parliament

The controversial law aimed at stamping out sectarianism around football games will be abolished, after every opposition party backed its repeal.

The Offensive Behaviour at Football and Threatening Communications Act 2012 (OBFA) was a casualty of the SNP losing its overall majority at Holyrood. Labour MSP James Kelly, who introduced a Member's Bill to repeal the OBFA in January 2017, confirmed he was delighted with the outcome. The Lib Dems and Greens, who stood on manifestos backing repeal, supported the plans. It left the SNP out-numbered 65–63 on the issue at Holyrood. Some SNP MSPs were also sceptical of the law, including Richard Lyle, who last year said it was 'too wide sweeping in approach and doesn't work in practice as well as it should or could'. The OBFA was created after a spate of violent incidents in the 2010–11 football season, including 35 arrests and a clash between club managers at an Old Firm game. Celtic manager Neil Lennon was targeted with parcel bombs and live bullets in the mail and lunged at by a Hearts fan at Tynecastle. The SNP rapidly pushed the OBFA through parliament, creating new offences around inciting religious hatred and offensive chanting associated with football. Only the SNP voted for it in December 2011 – it was opposed by all other parties, who complained the legislation was 'railroaded' using the SNP's then majority. Football fans claimed the law unfairly singled them out for blame and punishment.

Adapted from www.heraldscotland.com

Show your understanding

1. Create a spider diagram using the bullet pointed lists on the work MSPs do in parliament and in the constituency (page 88).
2. Explain the merits and limitations of FMQs in scrutinising the work of the government.
3. Why are written questions by MSPs a good way of holding the government to account?
4. a) What is a motion?
   b) How can a motion be used to hold the government to account?
5. a) What is a member's bill?
   b) Explain how James Kelly used his member's bill to hold the government to account.

Pressures on representatives

Like MPs, MSPs are public servants who are first and foremost elected to serve their constituents. However, they are also members of a political party and must ensure they support the party's policies. This can often cause conflict, especially when the MSP has to balance these pressures with their own personal beliefs and opinions.

MSP rebellions

Sometimes an MSP may disgree with the direction their party or party leader is going with a certain policy. This can be serious enough to result in the MSP rebelling against the party whip and voting against a particular policy. If the policy is a 'red-line issue' an MSP may feel completely at odds with their party's stance and decide to resign their party membership. (See the case study below.)

> ### Case study: Party loyalty versus personal beliefs – the Scottish government and NATO
>
> One of the most famous Scottish political rebellions in recent years came in the runup to the independence referendum when the SNP decided that, should Scotland ever become independent, then the country would apply to join NATO. This resulted in two SNP MSPs resigning in protest. John Finnie and Jean Urquhart, both MSPs in the Highlands, quit after the party very narrowly voted to overturn the decades-long ban on NATO membership. The MSPs insisted it was hypocritical and probably unworkable for the party to support the idea of Scotland joining a nuclear-armed military alliance while at the same time demanding that the UK removes the Trident nuclear weapons system from its base on the Clyde. John Finnie said, 'I cannot continue to belong to a party that quite rightly does not wish to hold nuclear weapons on its soil, but wants to join a first strike nuclear alliance. Although I envisage that I will continue to share common ground with the SNP on many issues, I cannot in good conscience continue to take the party whip. Jean Urquhart, who at the time had been a Campaign for Nuclear Disarmament member for 35 years, said, 'The issue of nuclear disarmament and removing Trident from Scotland's waters is a red-line issue for me, and I could not remain committed to a party that has committed itself to retaining membership of NATO.'

Lobbying

Lobbying is a controversial but important part of democratic politics. MSPs who are in power and therefore in a place to make decisions will be targeted by lobbyists (usually corporate businesses, industry bodies, think-tanks, law firms, management consultants and well-funded charities) whose paid job it is to influence the decisions taken by MSPs. Wherever there are politicians with the power to make decisions, there are lobbyists trying to influence those decisions. As the Scottish Parliament gets more powers, lobbying will increase. When the Scottish government passed the Alcohol (Minimum Pricing) (Scotland) Bill it faced a ferocious barrage of lobbying from the drinks industry, including the Scotch Whisky Association (SWA). The SWA has challenged the legislation all the way to the European Court of Justice.

Some argue that lobbying, especially by corporations, is controversial as it detracts from egalitarianism and may promote privileged access or, in extreme cases, corruption. As the Scottish Parliament regards itself as both modern and democratic, in 2016 it passed the Lobbying (Scotland) Bill, which creates a register of contacts who are paid to lobby MSPs in face-to-face meetings, events and hospitality occasions. Lobbyists are now required to register if they have met, or intend to meet, MSPs and are required to submit six-monthly returns of lobbying activity.

Tension between constituency and regional MSPs

Due to the workings of the additional member system (see Chapter 3) the traditional link between constituents and their representatives is now more complex. The constituency MSP represents a specific area and, having defeated other party candidates in a straightforward FPTP contest, they can claim to be the 'people's choice'. However, people are also represented by several regional MSPs. Both constituency and regional MSPs can come into conflict regarding each other's actions. Regional MSPs may be tempted to 'cherry pick' local issues with the purpose of winning the constituency seat at a future election. In contrast, constituency MSPs may regard their regional counterparts as less significant in the eyes of the constituents.

Show your understanding

1 Explain why party loyalty can sometimes be compromised. Refer to the case study.
2 a) What is lobbying?
   b) Why is lobbying controversial?
   c) What has the Scottish Parliament done to make lobbying more transparent?
3 Explain why there may be tension between constituency and regional MSPs.

Committees

Committees are small groups of MSPs who meet on a regular basis, usually on a Tuesday, Wednesday or Thursday morning, to scrutinise the work of the Scottish government, conduct inquiries into subjects within their remit and examine legislation. The committees play an important democratic role in the Scottish Parliament because, unlike the UK Parliament at Westminster, the Scottish Parliament is a single-chamber parliament, with no upper house or second chamber to scrutinise legislation. The Scottish Parliament's committee system allows for accessibility, openness and participation and it is generally accepted that the real work of the parliament is done in committee rooms. However, what makes the committee system at Holyrood even more open and accessible is the fact that it allows for the participation of as many people as possible in the democratic process. Committees often meet in public and can do so anywhere in Scotland, not just inside parliament. In fact, most committees allow the general public to attend and most committee meetings are streamed live on the Scottish Parliament website. This ensures transparency and can be said to represent democracy in action.

Types of committee

The parliament has different kinds of committee. Under parliamentary rules, it must establish mandatory committees. There are seven mandatory committees, including the Citizen Participation and Public Petitions Committee. It can also set up subject committees to look at specific subjects or areas of policy. There are currently nine subject committees that reflect the cabinet secretary portfolios. These include the Education, Children and Young People Committee and the Health, Social Care and Sport Committee. However, the parliament can also establish temporary committees on a short-term basis to consider particular issues. For example, in 2020, the COVID-19 Committee was established to consider and respond to the government's response to the COVID-19 pandemic. Subject committees may also include private bill committees, which are established to consider a particular bill that has been introduced by a person or body who is not an MSP.

Mandatory committees

- Citizen Participation and Public Petitions Committee
- Constitution, Europe, External Affairs and Culture Committee
- Delegated Powers and Law Reform Committee
- Equalities, Human Rights and Civil Justice Committee
- Finance and Public Administration Committee
- Public Audit Committee
- Standards and Procedures and Public Appointments Committee

Subject committees

- COVID-19 Recovery Committee
- Criminal Justice Committee
- Economy and Fair Work Committee
- Education, Children and Young People Committee
- Health, Social Care and Sport Committee
- Local Government, Housing and Planning Committee
- Net Zero, Energy and Transport Committee
- Rural Affairs, Islands and Natural Environment Committee
- Social Justice and Social Security Committee

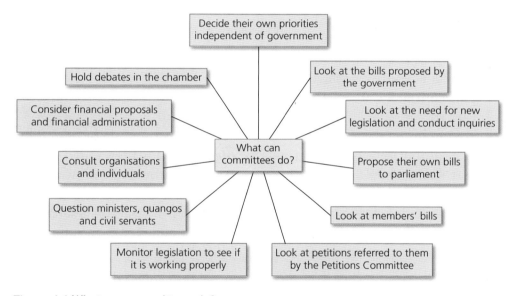

Figure 6.6 **What can committees do?**

Quango (Quasi-Autonomous Non-Governmental Organisation) – an organisation that is funded by taxpayers, but not controlled directly by central government.

Committee membership

The Scottish Parliament is a relatively small parliament of 129 MSPs and committee membership is restricted to MSPs who are not in the government. Most committees have between 7 and 11 members, depending on the role and remit of the committee. The appointment of members takes account of the balance of the various political parties and groupings in the parliament, with all MSPs normally being on at least one committee but occasionally two. The Parliamentary Bureau can also recommend changes to the membership or make-up of committees. As committees comprise various political party members this should, in theory, ensure rigorous debate, scrutiny and accountability.

> The Parliamentary Bureau is a group of MSPs representing political parties and groupings with five or more MSPs in the parliament. They meet regularly to discuss the parliament's business and propose its business programme.

All committees are chaired by a convener and meet regularly – either weekly or fortnightly, depending on their workload. The members of the committee choose a convener from a political party following a recommendation by the Parliamentary Bureau (based on party numbers in parliament). In addition, each committee normally has a deputy convener who chairs meetings in the convener's absence. Deputy conveners are chosen in the same way as conveners. These are important roles because conveners can set the committee agenda, steering what is discussed and – sometimes more importantly – what is not discussed. Ordinary committee members can raise issues during meetings and get their concerns recorded. They can also attend and speak at any committee meetings, including those of which they are not a member, but they can only vote in their own committees. Because of the strength of party discipline, committee members usually follow their party line, but there is sometimes a conflict of interest between their constituents' views, their party line and their own personal interests (see page 99). As the SNP hold 64 seats in parliament they therefore dominate committee membership. The SNP still convene 8 out of 16 committees which gives them control over the agenda of those committees.

The work of committees

Figure 6.7 **A Scottish Parliamentary Committee meeting**

Committees have two key functions – to scrutinise the work of the Scottish government and to examine legislation. The majority of committees' work is carried out when they have to:

- scrutinise the activities of the Scottish government
- scrutinise a proposal or draft bill
- investigate a matter
- decide whether to propose a committee bill
- consider a bill
- consider proposals for members' bills
- consider and report on subordinate legislation.

Their work involves the following areas.

Legislation

Every piece of legislation coming out of Holyrood will have come under the scrutiny of one or more of the Scottish Parliament's committees; therefore, it is through the function of committees that the Scottish government is held to account by the parliament. Out of the three stages in the passage of a bill, the legislation is scrutinised by a committee at two of them (stages 1 and 2) before the whole parliament debates and votes on whether to pass it at stage 3 (see Figure 6.4 on page 86).

> **Subordinate legislation** – an Act (primary legislation) may delegate power to a government minister to make orders, regulations or rules relating to the Act. This is known as subordinate (or secondary) legislation. Often, the details of an Act – for example, those concerning timing, implementation or the mechanism for updating – are left to subordinate legislation.

Inquiries

Committees can investigate any area that is within their remit and affects the people of Scotland, and can publish a report setting out their recommendations. Past inquiry reports have included food bank funding and eating disorders. These reports are normally discussed at a meeting of the full parliament, and as a consequence have influenced government policies and resulted in changes to legislation. Inquiries can also be conducted into how legislation passed by the parliament has worked in practice – this is sometimes referred to as 'post-legislative scrutiny'. In some cases, committees will wish to bring areas of Scottish government policy under detailed scrutiny and hold ministers to account. Committees will invite witnesses to give evidence at an inquiry. These could be cabinet secretaries, ministers or other people who may have knowledge or expertise that could assist the committee's work. In 2016 the Infrastructure and Capital Investment Committee held an inquiry into the circumstances surrounding the closure of the Forth Road Bridge in late 2015. Specifically, the remit of the inquiry was: 'To examine the management, monitoring and maintenance of the Forth Road Bridge principally in the 10-year period prior to its closure on public safety grounds in December 2015.' This inquiry put the SNP administration under intense scrutiny as the government made budget cuts and cancelled maintenance in the years preceding the closure.

In 2018, the Education and Skills Committee conducted an inquiry into the possible narrowing of subject choices in secondary education. They heard evidence from teachers, parents, universities, Education Scotland, trade unions and many other interested parties. In concluding their inquiry in late 2019 their report recommended the following:

'A review of the senior phase of curriculum for excellence is needed to ensure that pupil aspirations are being met and that breadth of opportunity remain a cornerstone of Scottish education.

This is just one of the recommendations of a report issued today by the Scottish Parliament's Education and Skills Committee following an inquiry on the number of subjects available to pupils in secondary school and in particular concerns regarding reduction in subject choice at S4.

The Committee heard that following the introduction of the Curriculum for Excellence, which changed the way education is delivered in Scotland's schools, there has been confusion and inadequate support from Education Scotland and SQA [Scottish Qualifications Authority].

This report asks the Scottish Government to commission an independent review of the senior phase of Scottish education, which takes place from S4–S6, to find out how the concerns expressed to the Committee during the inquiry can be addressed.'

Following this recommendation, the cabinet secretary for education and skills, John Swinney, announced that an independent review would be commissioned with the aim of improving subject choice in S4–S6.

In 2020–21, the most high-profile and controversial committee inquiry took place. A special subject committee was set up to look into the Scottish government's handling of harassment claims against former first minister,

Alex Salmond. During the inquiry, Nicola Sturgeon and other senior ministers appeared at the committee to give evidence. Sturgeon was grilled for eight hours during her sitting.

Other areas

Committees can also consider and report on government policy and actions, on European legislation, on secondary (or subordinate) legislation and on public petitions concerning the people of Scotland.

Citizen Participation and Public Petitions Committee

The Citizen Participation and Public Petitions Committee is the main way for members of the public to influence government policy in Holyrood. The committee considers petitions and makes a decision on the course of action to be taken in each case. The Citizen Participation and Public Petitions Committee has several courses of

action it may take. It decides whether the parliament as a whole should debate the issue, whether a specific committee should deal with it or whether it is more appropriate for another body to consider the petition. All committees have a responsibility to consider and report on petitions sent to them. Petitions are submitted by individuals and groups who want to raise an issue and many petitions are driven by the experience of petitioners at a local level – for example, a campaign to stop a local school closure or prevent development on a local playing field. While the Citizen Participation and Public Petitions Committee cannot become directly involved in such matters it can ask the Scottish government to review the wider national policies and/or guidance that govern the actions of local authorities and other public bodies. The public petitions system is a key part of the Scottish Parliament's commitment to openness and accessibility. Petitions can have positive outcomes that lead to change or inform debate – the smoking ban was first raised as a public petition.

Case study: Committee achievements in challenging government and influencing policy (parliamentary session 5, 2016–21)

- The UNCRC Bill was passed by the Scottish Parliament on 16 March 2021. The legislation makes children and young people's rights justiciable under Scots law. The Equalities and Human Rights Committee was at the forefront of constructing the bill.
- The Education and Skills Committee carried out 20 inquiries in session 5. Several of their inquiries resulted in significant progress being made. For example, recommendations made in their report on subject choices in Senior Phase education in Scotland led directly to the establishment of the OECD's review of the Curriculum for Excellence in late 2019. The review's initial remit, which was to consider the operation of the Senior Phase, was expanded in 2020 to cover the whole Curriculum for Excellence and following the 2020 SQA exam results was further expanded to cover the assessment and qualifications approach in the Senior Phase.
- The COVID-19 Committee's work included a focus on the Scottish government's long-term strategy for responding to COVID-19 beyond 2021. This work was encapsulated in the Committee's 'next steps' inquiry. The Committee took evidence from experts in epidemiology who had experience from Scotland, Hong Kong and New Zealand. This enabled the Committee to gain international perspectives on approaches to tackling COVID-19, to hear expert opinions on the future course of the pandemic and to consider what could be learned from previous pandemics. The inquiry was shared with the Scottish government.

Source: © Parliamentary copyright. Scottish Parliament Corporate Body

Case study: Does the Scottish Parliament scrutinise legislation effectively enough?

The Scottish Parliament was designed to be a powerful and effective legislature with committees at the heart of its work. This aim was outlined in the final report of the Scottish Constitutional Convention, which expected a 'parliament to operate through a system of powerful committees which are able to initiate legislation as well as to scrutinise and amend government proposals, and which have wide-ranging investigative functions'. The parliament has combined standing and select committee functions to help develop expertise within the committees responsible for scrutinising legislation. Most committees are permanent and not subject to government dissolution. They have relatively few members to allow them to develop a 'businesslike', not partisan, culture. The number of conveners (chairs) is proportional by party and they are selected by each committee. Committee deliberation takes place before the initial and final plenary stages. Committees can invite witnesses and demand government documents and they have an unusual role which involves the monitoring of the Scottish government's pre-legislative consultation. Further, if all else fails, they have the ability to initiate their own bills (as can individual MSPs) in a much more straightforward way than in Westminster.

However, the Scottish Parliament was not designed to be a powerful legislature in the way that we associate with political systems such as that in the USA. Crucially, there are not the same divisions of powers and checks and balances between executive, legislature and judiciary. Instead, the executive operates at the heart of the legislature and, when enjoying a single or coalition party majority, has the ability to control its procedures. Furthermore, committees are said to be hamstrung by the amount of legislation they have to scrutinise with most bills being fairly innocuous and receiving cross-party support. This means that committees rarely set the agenda for future Scottish government action by, for example, identifying gaps in existing policy and prompting further action by introducing committee bills. In relation to this, when it comes to conducting inquiries, many inquiries have been charged with partisanship and do not produce meaningful advice and engagement with government. As mentioned earlier, the SNP dominates committee membership and convenorship, and MSPs toe the party line. Lastly, effective scrutiny requires the Scottish Parliament to have a sufficient number of staff able to devote their time and attention to the policy work and legislation of the Scottish government. However, the Scottish Parliament employs relatively few relevant staff compared to Westminster.

Source: Adapted from a paper by Paul Cairney of Stirling University

ICT task

Visit the Scottish Parliament website and research the current petitions being considered by the Citizen Participation and Public Petitions Committee.

Added Value idea

The scrutinising powers of the Scottish Parliament have come under criticism for being inadequate. Research options such as increasing the size of parliament or introducing a second chamber.

Show your understanding

1 What is a committee?
2 Describe the two different types of committee.
3 Describe the membership set-ups of committees.
4 Why is the role of convener important?
5 Describe the work of committees in scrutinising the government regarding:
   a) legislation
   b) inquiries.
6 Explain the role and remit of the Citizen Participation and Public Petitions Committee.
7 Read the case study on the effectiveness of parliament scrutiny. In 150 words summarise the ways in which the Scottish Parliament is effective and not effective when it comes to scrutinising the government.

12-mark question

Evaluate the effectiveness of parliamentary representatives in holding the government to account.

20-mark question

Parliament has had little success in holding the government to account. Discuss.

7 Representative democracy in the UK

As mentioned in Chapter 1, the UK's political system is a parliamentary democracy with a constitutional monarchy in which the country is managed by a process involving elected representatives and various institutions. These institutions work together in maintaining, developing and creating new laws that drive forward change. Judgement of the success and/or failures of these changes usually takes place every five years when most of the UK's citizens vote in a general election. Following this election, it is often the case that new representatives are elected as MPs and a new government is formed to drive forward further change.

The role of political representatives

Each MP represents all of the people within their constituency regardless of whether they voted for them or not. Additionally, MPs are usually also members of a political party and so are expected to support their party leader and the party's policies. This can cause conflict at times, especially if policies have negative effects on their constituents. However, voters vote not only for the individual but also because of their affiliation with a party and so MPs are expected by constituents to support the aims of the party as well.

The majority of MPs are known as 'backbenchers'. This means that they have not been promoted to the government or shadow government. These backbenchers have many opportunities to influence the decision-making process. When in parliament, MPs carry out some of the following roles:

- Asking government ministers questions on behalf of their constituents or other interested organisations. On most occasions this will take the form of written questions, and government ministers must respond to these. This can be at any ministers' questions sessions, or by sending internal emails/letters to a government department.
- Debating on key issues affecting the country and on legislation that may be passing through parliament. This can take the form of a debate in the Westminster Hall or adjournment debates of the Commons chamber.
- As members of committees, carrying out a number of duties including meetings, interviewing key stakeholders and other correspondence.
- Creating their own Early Day Motions, which highlight issues that may lead on to a debate in the chamber, and also on occasion creating a Private Members' Bill that if selected by ballot can become an Act of Parliament.
- Lastly, and most crucially, voting on legislation. All MPs have one vote each and so during voting within the chamber (sometimes referred to as divisions) all MPs, in theory, have equal power.

Representation

A key issue with parliament is whether it accurately represents the population of the UK. One criticism is of the social class and educational background of MPs. After the general election in 2019 it was found that 29 per cent of MPs went to a fee-paying school, even though these schools educate just 7 per cent of the population. Also, one in ten of these privately educated MPs went to the same secondary school – Eton. Boris Johnson is the twentieth prime minister to have been educated at Eton. Of the 427 winning candidates who went to university, 137 (21 per cent) went to either Oxford or Cambridge University. Although these universities are attended by students from a range of backgrounds (and in fact, both now admit more students from state than private schools), the student body has traditionally not been as socially diverse as at some other UK universities. After the last election it was noted that 27 per cent of all Tory MPs and 18 per cent of Labour MPs had been to Oxbridge. According to Rebecca Montacute from the Sutton Trust, the educational background of MPs matters because 'if MPs come from very different backgrounds to the general public, there is a risk that the concerns and priorities of all parts of society will not be adequately reflected in parliament.'

In addition to social background, the number of female MPs is also an issue for the House of Commons. Traditionally, women have been greatly under-represented in Westminster. In 1979 only 19 MPs were women. However, since then the situation has significantly improved (see Table 7.1). The number of female MPs rose from 147 (22 per cent) in 2010 to 220 (34 per cent) in 2019. The Conservatives and Labour both witnessed a jump in the number of female MPs, and the SNP also brought 16 female MPs into the mix. In 2019, for the first time, the number of Labour and Liberal Democrat female MPs outnumbered male. However, the House of

Commons compares poorly in this respect to Rwanda (63.1 per cent), Sweden (46.1 per cent) and South Africa (42.7 per cent).

Table 7.1 Gender and ethnic background of MPs 1987–2019

	Gender		Ethnic background	
	Male	Female	White	BAME
1987	609	41 (6%)	646	4 (0.6%)
1992	591	60 (9%)	645	6 (0.9%)
1997	539	120 (18%)	650	9 (1.4%)
2001	541	118 (18%)	647	12 (1.8%)
2005	518	128 (20%)	631	15 (2.3%)
2010	507	143 (22%)	623	27 (4.2%)
2015	459	191 (29%)	608	41 (6.6%)
2017	442	208 (32%)	598	52 (8%)
2019	430	220 (33.8%)	585	65 (10%)

Source: UK Parliament

The 2019 general election also witnessed improvements for the representation of MPs from a BAME background in Westminster. BAME MPs made up more than 10 per cent of the 2019 parliament, up from 4.2 per cent in 2010. Now 63 minority-ethnic MPs sit in the Commons, building on the success of the 2010 election, when 27 BAME MPs won seats in Westminster. Among them is Sarah Owen, the MP for Luton North, who is the first Labour MP of East Asian origin and first female MP of Chinese origin.

Lastly, the age of MPs has also been a source of criticism. The average age of MPs in 2019 was 50 years of age and this is consistent with previous parliaments. Indeed since 1979 the lowest average age has been 49 and the highest 51. This is despite the influx of younger SNP MPs such as Mhairi Black MP for Paisley and Renfrewshire South, who became the youngest ever UK parliamentarian at only 20 years of age.

Figure 7.1 Mhairi Black MP (above) and Sarah Owen MP (below)

Show your understanding

1 Describe the UK's political system.
2 Explain the role of a political representative.
3 Why are most MPs known as 'backbenchers'?
4 Summarise the main tasks that MPs undertake in parliament.

Develop your skills

'Parliament is not accurately representative of the UK but is making improvements.' To what extent do you agree with this statement?

ICT task

Look online to see what activities in parliament your local MP has been involved in over the last month. Summarise your findings in a detailed paragraph. You can check official parliament records or look on your MP's social media platforms such as Twitter and Facebook.

Limitations on MPs

Party loyalty

At the centre of the debate over party loyalty is the fact that MPs must balance their role as representatives of citizens with the aims of their political party. One key aspect of the workings of parliament is political parties' use of the 'whip' system. It is the job of party whips to enforce strong party discipline. The party whip ensures that MPs toe the party line and drives rebellious or straying MPs back into line with the party. Whips also act as tellers by counting votes in divisions and organising the pairing system, whereby pairs of opposing MPs both agree not to vote when either is prevented from being at Westminster.

The big dilemma for MPs arises when there is a conflict of interest. In most cases, MPs do as their party wishes and vote when and as instructed by the whips.

Loyalty and toeing the party line can lead to reward and promotion, whereas disloyalty can lead to sanctions and ultimately removal from the party – this is known as 'withdrawing the whip' and while it does not result in the MP losing their job (they were after all given the job by their constituents) it can mean that in the next election they will not be the party's chosen candidate and so stand little chance of winning their seat again. This is also the case where the MP embarrasses the party by being accused of acting immorally or illegally.

The job of the whips becomes more important if the majority of the party in government is small or when a coalition is formed, because this can make it more likely that the government will lose major votes. Therefore, it is crucial that both government and opposition whips get as many of their MPs to vote as possible, and with their party.

Backbench rebellions

A key measure of how much power a government has is the number of backbench MPs who rebel against the whip and vote against their wishes. During Theresa May's last few months and Boris Johnson's first few months as prime minister there was a record number of rebellious votes where Conservative MPs voted against government bills. This was due to the controversy over the UK's exit from Europe.

Rebellious MPs are a common feature of the UK Parliament. According to website publicwhip.org.uk, from 2010 to 2015, coalition MPs rebelled in a record 35 per cent of divisions. That easily beats the previous record of 28 per cent, held by the Blair/Brown government from 2005 to 2010.

Table 7.2 The House of Commons' most rebellious MPs since 2017

Kate Hoey (Labour)	46.6%
Frank Field (lost seat in 2019) (Labour)	28.8%
Graham Stringer (Labour)	28.2%
Kenneth Clarke (retired 2019) (Conservative)	26.4%

Source: publicwhip.org.uk

Show your understanding

1 Explain the role of party whips.
2 In what ways can a party punish MPs who defy their wishes?
3 What are backbench rebellions?
4 Why did the Conservative governments in 2019 suffer a record number of backbench rebellions?

The Legislature and Executive in the UK

People often confuse parliament with government and vice versa. While they work hand-in-glove with each other in the creation of laws, they are completely separate institutions.

The government runs the country by driving forward its ideas and attempting to turn them into new bills and by implementing its own policies. Thus the government can also be referred to as the Executive. Parliament essentially acts as a 'checkpoint' for the government by ensuring that the work of government is scrutinised, people are held to account and bills are thoroughly examined and finally approved into law. Parliament is the highest legislative authority in the UK and so is referred to as the Legislature. Although it is not part of the making of laws, a key element in the evaluation of government policy is the Judiciary. These are the courts that often process the government acts and controversially can challenge the Executive and Legislature on occasion.

The Legislature

The UK Parliament is made up of three parts: the House of Commons, the House of Lords and the monarch (the king or queen). All three institutions combine to carry out the work of parliament. The Legislature in the UK is bicameral. This means that legislative business takes place in two chambers or houses: the House of Commons and the House of Lords.

Legislation

The primary function of parliament is to make laws and change existing laws (legislation). However, a new law must pass through and complete a series of stages in both the House of Commons and the House of Lords, with mutual agreement by both, before it is finally approved.

A bill, which can begin in either house, is a proposal for a new law or a proposal to change an existing law and is debated in parliament. Either house can vote down a bill, in which case it will normally not become law, but there are exceptions. The Commons can pass the same bill in two successive years, in which case it can become law without the agreement of the Lords. Bills that are only about money (raising taxes or authorising government expenditure) are usually not opposed in the Lords and may only be delayed for a month. The monarch must approve the bill by signing it – this is known as royal assent. At this point, the bill becomes an Act of Parliament and is a law.

The process by which a bill becomes a law is characterised by a series of debates, scrutiny and amendment. The complete process is explained here.

White paper: This contains the government's idea for a bill. It is written to allow discussion and consultation with interested parties before the idea becomes a bill.

First reading: The bill is read or introduced to parliament without a debate or vote taking place.

Second reading: The bill is debated and must be approved in a vote to proceed.

Committee stage: The bill goes through detailed scrutiny by an all-party Public Bill Committee and amendments are made, if required.

Report stage: The whole House of Commons considers any amendments made by the Committee and can accept, alter or reject them.

Third reading: The amended bill is debated but cannot be amended again at this stage. A vote is taken on whether to accept the amended bill.

If the amended bill passes this stage it goes to the House of Lords, where the whole process is repeated. If the Lords amend the bill further, it is returned to the Commons for approval; at this point, the amendments made by the Lords may be accepted, rejected or changed by the House of Commons. This can lead to what is known as 'parliamentary ping-pong', as a bill is bounced back and forth between the two houses. Ultimately though, if agreement cannot be reached it is the Commons that has the greater power. It can accept the Lords' amendments, drop the bill altogether or invoke the Parliament Act.

Once the various stages of the bill's passing through parliament have taken place there is then a final vote by MPs on whether to pass the finalised bill on to royal assent and therefore make it an Act of Parliament.

The two most important stages in the passage of a bill are the second reading and the committee stage. During the second reading, the principle of the bill is debated and at this stage it is vulnerable to being thrown out after a vote by the House. At the committee stage, the Public Bill Committee – which is made up of a majority of government MPs and may include party whips – can usually ensure a safe passage for the bill. By having this majority on the committee the government is usually able to squeeze through its bill with minimal changes. As we see later, the size of the government's majority is a key aspect of getting its proposed bill through parliament safely.

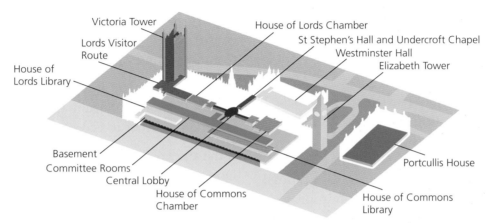

Figure 7.2 The Houses of Parliament, the House of Commons, the House of Lords, Westminster Hall and the committee rooms

The House of Commons

Known as the lower chamber, the House of Commons is where most of the high-profile activity takes place in parliament. In this chamber all elected MPs work for their constituents and hold the government to account. Since 2010 there have been 650 MPs representing the constituencies of the entire UK, although this number has fluctuated in the past and will likely do so in the future due mainly to population changes. This is a form of indirect democracy and in essence ensures that all citizens are represented in parliament. The main roles of the House of Commons can be summed up in the following ways:

- the passing of legislation
- the scrutiny of those in power.

The passing of legislation

As shown earlier in the chapter, the House of Commons plays a key role in the passing of legislation. In fact, it is the dominant chamber, given that the government itself usually holds the balance of power in the chamber. When this is the case, the government can rely on their own MPs to help push through their plans. Following the 2019 general election, the Conservative Party held the balance of power as they had a majority of MPs (365). This was one of the biggest majorities a government has ever had (80 more MPs than all the other parties added together) and gave them a majority of MPs in the chamber as well as a majority on many of the committees that scrutinise the work of the government.

The vast majority of bills that are processed through parliament are introduced by the government. Following the 2019 general election, the UK government proposed a number of bills relating to Brexit (the UK's departure from the EU), a Counter-Terrorism and Sentencing Bill and a new Environment Bill.

> ## ICT task
>
> Go to http://services.parliament.uk/bills to check on the current status of the bills that are passing through parliament.

Tony Blair's Labour government was able to pass all government bills between its election in 1997 and 2005 owing to its large majority of MPs. However, the Conservative–Liberal Democrat coalition government suffered a record number of defeats of its bills between 2010 and 2015, which is perhaps indicative of the fact that it had to share a majority and many disagreements took place as bills passed through parliament. With a majority of 80 MPs, Boris Johnson's government following the 2019 general election are highly unlikely to suffer a defeat in their bills. Any potential dissent or rebellion from its own MPs will make the government listen. However, it is likely that any amendments will be agreed before the bill is presented for its first reading.

Private Members' Bills

Apart from government bills, there are limited opportunities for individual MPs to put forward their own ideas. If they receive enough sponsorship, and they are successfully drawn out of a ballot, they might find that their own bill begins its passage through parliament. For the 2015–16 session only 20 Private Members' Bills were drawn for consideration in parliament. Of course, individual MPs do not necessarily have the support of the majority of MPs so more often than not these bills do not make it all the way through parliament. However, there are a number of examples of a Private Members' Bill becoming an Act of Parliament.

- Murder (Abolition of the Death Penalty) Act 1965: Introduced by Sydney Silverman, who was the MP for the Nelson and Colne constituency in Lancashire, it effectively ended the death penalty in Great Britain, replacing it with a sentence of life imprisonment.
- The Assaults on Emergency Workers (Offences) Act 2019 was introduced by Christopher Bryant, who is the MP for Rhondda in Wales. The Act was passed after a growing concern about assaults on emergency workers. The Act resulted in a possible sentence of up to 12 months for assaulting an emergency worker, double what was available to judges previously.

Scrutiny of government actions

Perhaps the most important role of the House of Commons is to scrutinise the work of the government. The MPs in the chamber represent every single citizen of the UK and so on their behalf they 'check' that the government is working in the best interests of all. Therefore, the Executive is accountable to the general public.

There are a number of processes in place in parliament to examine the work of the government. The main way in which MPs scrutinise policy is through questioning government ministers, debating current issues and policy and the investigative work of committees. The government can publicly respond to explain and justify its policies and decisions.

Questions

MPs can ask questions of government ministers. The majority of questions asked receive written answers, but some are answered orally for around an hour each day from Monday to Thursday on the floor of the House. For example, the secretary of state for business, energy and industrial strategy answers questions on Tuesdays at 12.15 p.m. The most high profile of these sessions is Prime Minister's Question Time (PMQs), which takes place each Wednesday at noon for 30 minutes. These sessions provide an opportunity for the shadow opposition ministers and backbench MPs (selected by the speaker) to 'grill' the prime minister or minister about their policies or actions. A large section of this session is given over to the leader of the opposition, who will try to expose a policy flaw or failure and challenge the government to answer important questions. A common critique of PMQs is that it can be drawn into an aggressive shouting match, with both sides jeering from the backbenches. This is known as 'Punch and Judy politics'. Another criticism of PMQs is that it lacks effectiveness, with the prime minister only being able to give short answers as time is severely limited. However, it does give MPs direct access to those with the most power in government.

Figure 7.3 Prime Minister's Question Time

Debates

At the end of each day's business, the House adjourns (suspends) proceedings until the following day's sitting with a half-hour adjournment debate. This gives MPs an opportunity to discuss government policy, proposed new laws and current issues, but also to raise issues of concern and interest to their constituents. These debates are designed to help MPs reach an informed decision on a subject but are often poorly attended. Since 1999 'Westminster Hall' debates have taken place to allow MPs more time to debate big issues. For example, in March 2020 there was a debate on the issue of the mental health of military veterans and the relevant services available in the UK. A regular criticism of these debates is that they often have very low attendance and may not lead to any meaningful changes in government policy.

ICT task

Visit http://calendar.parliament.uk/ to have a look at what has gone on in parliament over the past week or so.

Show your understanding

1 Why is a majority important in the House of Commons?
2 What are some of the government bills currently making their way through parliament?
3 Explain, in detail, the features of a Private Members' Bill.
4 Describe some of the criticisms of ministers' questions and debates.

Select committees

Each government minister is shadowed by an MP from the opposition whose job it is to scrutinise their work. The work of their department is also checked by a group of MPs. These groups are known as select committees and their role is to scrutinise the work of all major government departments and concentrate on expenditure, policies and administration. Select committees are widely accepted as the most effective means of parliamentary scrutiny of the Executive and the decision-making process. Each has 11 backbench MP members who are elected by their own party. The select committee system allows for the questioning of ministers and forces them to explain themselves.

Issues with select committees

Select committee membership reflects the composition of the House of Commons, and so a government with a majority in the House also has a majority on committees. This has led to criticisms from some commentators that these MPs will put their allegiance to the government before the important job of scrutinising the Executive. As some MPs seek promotion through the ranks of their party they may be reluctant to expose malpractice or irregularities in the government of which they wish to be a part. Also, they cannot compel the government to follow their recommendations. This had led some to describe select committees as 'watchdogs without teeth'. However, a 2019 report found that the recommendations of committees regularly impact on legislation passing through parliament. For example, the Health and Social Care Committee held a follow-up inquiry into childhood obesity, which was instrumental in persuading the government to publish a 'Chapter 2' to its childhood obesity strategy and implement many of the committee's ten key recommendations. Also, committees are said to play an important part in deterring the government from introducing unpopular policies which might damage the Executive's reputation with the public. Select committees have also made headline news by scrutinising some very influential people. In July 2011 Rupert and James Murdoch gave evidence to the Culture, Media and Sport Select Committee as it began its investigation into phone hacking (see case study).

Meanwhile executives from Starbucks, Google and Amazon gave evidence to the Public Account Committee, which led to Google announcing in January 2016 that it would pay £130 million in backdated tax to HMRC. In 2018 Mark Zuckerberg was summoned by the Digital, Culture, Media and Sport Committee as part of its investigation into Facebook's role in the Cambridge Analytica scandal.

In 2006, Public Bill Committees were introduced in place of standing committees to scrutinise legislation. Unlike standing committees, they act in a similar way to select committees: they can call forward witnesses to obtain evidence on the bills and request written information from any interested parties, thereby adding 'teeth' to their legislative scrutiny and its potential impact. However, their composition still reflects the proportion of the parties in parliament, meaning that the government retains a majority on each committee – easing the passage of bills.

The Backbench Business Committee gives backbench MPs the power to call for debates in the chamber and in Westminster Hall at least once a week. It is also responsible for parliament's e-petitions website: in an e-petition, any member of the public can highlight an issue and, if the petition gains more than 100,000 signatures, the committee will hear the argument for it to be debated by MPs. In January 2016, following an e-petition signed by more than 575,000 people, the House of Commons debated on whether to ban controversial American businessman Donald Trump from entering the UK and in February 2017 an e-petition was signed by over 1.8 million people to ban President Trump from making an official state visit once he was sworn in. While many MPs did argue for this ban, the majority decided that it was not in the UK's interest to ban President Trump.

Case study: Select committee on phone hacking

In 2011 the Culture, Media and Sport Select Committee held an inquiry into allegations made against the *News of the World* newspaper that it had, over a number of years, been hacking into the voicemails of politicians, celebrities and sports stars. Famous people such as Prince William, actress Scarlett Johansson and footballer David Beckham are thought to have had their phones hacked during this period. The committee, chaired by Conservative MP John Whittingdale, included ten other MPs.

The committee called upon *News of the World* owner Rupert Murdoch, his son James Murdoch and chief executive Rebekah Brooks. It was during one of these meetings that a protestor called Jonnie Marbles attacked Rupert Murdoch with a foam pie, which triggered a huge security alert. The protestor shouted that Murdoch was a 'naughty billionaire', indicating that he disapproved of his company's alleged phone-hacking practices.

After hearing the three witnesses, including particularly strong questioning from Labour MP Tom Watson, it was revealed that the voicemail of schoolgirl Milly Dowler, who had been murdered in 2002, had been hacked and her messages listened to while she was missing, which had given false hope to her parents and to the police that she was still alive.

As a result of the investigation the *News of the World* was closed down and Rebekah Brooks lost her job. The committee recommended to the House of Commons that a judicial inquiry should take place into ethics within the media. This was known as the Leveson Inquiry, which has made wide-ranging recommendations, including the creation of an independent body to monitor press standards which should be backed by legislation.

Backbench Business Committee

Set up in June 2010, the aim of the Backbench Business Committee (BBBC) is to give backbench MPs greater control over the Executive. The committee has eight members from across the main political parties. It meets on Tuesdays to consider requests for debates on any subject from MPs. Journalist Quentin Letts has described this process as being like the TV programme *Dragons' Den,* with backbench MPs having to pitch issues to the committee. This is seen as being much more open and transparent than the previous system, where the government decided on debates and scheduled all business behind closed doors. Thus more power is now with backbench MPs.

Debates initiated by the BBBC

September 2011 Motion calling for the continued deployment of UK armed forces in Afghanistan. This forced the government to allow MPs to vote on this issue, resulting in the eventual withdrawal of UK troops.

January 2013 Motion to reduce the voting age to 16. This was the first time that MPs had voted on this issue and the motion was passed, putting it on the agenda despite government opposition to the idea.

March 2015 Motion to stop the badger cull. This vote signalled cross-party opposition to the government's policy. It forced the government into taking a stance on the issue and put it into the public agenda.

While the BBBC has ensured that issues important to backbench MPs are put on the agenda there have been a number of criticisms. As the membership of the committee is severely limited, parties outside of the 'big two' usually have only one representative. In 2012 the coalition government changed the way in which members are elected. Previously, the whole house elected members but, following a 'whipped' vote, and despite the protestations of the committee itself, it is now party whips who select their members. This was seen as a demonstration of Executive dominance and brought accusations that the BBBC now offers less robust scrutiny of the work of the government. In June 2020 the BBBC debated the impact of COVID-19 on BAME communities and produced a report for the UK government.

Figure 7.4 A Backbench Business Committee meeting

ICT task

Go to https://petition.parliament.uk

Look at some of the recent open petitions. If a petition has more than 100,000 signatures then the BBBC will hear the arguments for it to be scheduled into parliamentary business. Make a short profile of a petition that interests you. If you feel strongly then why not sign it yourself!

Show your understanding

1 Describe the main features of select committees.
2 Explain some of the limitations of select committees.
3 'The Backbench Business Committee gives backbench MPs more power.' To what extent is this statement accurate?
4 Give details of the select committee on phone hacking.

Reform of the House of Commons

As with any political institution, the House of Commons should constantly look to change for the better, including staying up to date with the way that the public shows their interest in politics and also the accountability of its members. One criticism of the House of Commons is the way that it is perceived by the general public. Its processes are seen as archaic and generally out of step with modern life. To combat this there have been a number of procedural changes brought about by the recommendations of the Wright Committee that were adopted by the coalition government of 2010–15. These reforms included giving backbenchers more say in setting the House's agenda and the establishment of the BBBC (see page 109). Further reforms include the introduction of elections for chairs and members of select committees and improvements in the petitions system.

While these changes have largely taken place some still think that more changes are needed.

For example, in December 2015 the SNP called for electronic voting as, under the current arrangements, each vote can take up to 20 minutes to process. The SNP has called this a 'waste of time' and called for an end to the 'antiquated Westminster tradition'. In June 2020, the SNP continued to question these traditions by requesting that voting in the chamber be completed remotely due to the COVID-19 outbreak. However, parliament continued to sit and if MPs wanted to vote to accept or reject legislation they had to attend. For one piece of legislation it took 46 minutes for the vote to take place due to social-distancing rules.

Show your understanding

1 Give details of some of the criticisms of the House of Commons.
2 With a partner, list some of the possible ways in which you think parliament could modernise itself.

The House of Lords

The House of Lords plays a key role in the legislative process. It debates and scrutinises bills as they pass through parliament, helping to ensure that legislation is well drafted and effective. It makes laws, holds the government to account and investigates policy issues. The people who sit in the House of Lords, unlike members of the House of Commons, are not elected and not paid a salary. There are currently around 800 members, known as lords or peers, making the chamber one of the largest legislative bodies in the world after China's National People's Congress. There are three different types of member: life peers, hereditary peers (whose titles are inherited through their family and given up upon their death) and bishops. The majority of lords are life peers, chosen because of the work they have done throughout their careers. This can include people such as athletes, actors, scientists, doctors, politicians, lawyers and writers. This expertise is seen as a key asset to parliament.

Figure 7.5 Michelle Mone, Scottish businesswoman made a peer in 2015

Making laws

Nearly all bills have to pass through both the Commons and the Lords prior to becoming Acts of Parliament. Bills (draft laws) are debated and scrutinised in both houses.

Legislation takes up about 60 per cent of the House of Lords' time, and members are involved throughout the process of proposing, revising and amending legislation.

Peers scrutinise the government over Brexit deal

In January 2020 Boris Johnson's Brexit deal was defeated three times in a single day in the House of Lords.

The European Union (Withdrawal Agreement) Bill took a drubbing as peers voted to amend clauses around the post-Brexit rights of EU citizens, specifically the right to a physical form of proof of status.

The government was first defeated when peers voted by a majority of 41 to allow EU citizens physical proof of their settled status.

Shortly after, by a majority of 36, peers voted to remove that power from the Bill, upon concern that it might be seen to interfere with the independence of the judiciary.

The third defeat for the government came as Lords voted to allow cases to be referred to the Supreme Court to decide whether to depart from EU case law.

After this pummelling in the Lords, the Bill will now return to the Commons, where the prime minister will have no concern in overturning it.

The Bill had previously flown through the Commons with large majorities. With the clock ticking to Brexit day on 31 January, peers did not accept that they were challenging Brexit or attempting to stymie the legislation.

Liberal Democrat Lord Oates said he did not agree with the government's proposals that EU citizens under the settled status scheme should have only digital proof of status.

Lord McNicol of West Kilbride reiterated his opposition and said he would continue to vote against the government unless concessions were made.

Scrutinising the work of the government

Lords check the work of the government by questioning and debating decisions made by ministers and government departments. About 40 per cent of their time is spent on scrutiny.

The House of Lords plays a vital role in scrutinising the work of the government and holding it to account for its decisions and activities. With government ministers sitting in the House and many former ministers, senior politicians and officials among its membership, the House of Lords is well placed to question the government with rigour and insight. Because its members do not represent constituencies they therefore do not need to satisfy the wishes of voters, and are not subject to pressure from whips, meaning that they can speak and vote freely on issues.

They can also debate controversial issues that are generally avoided by the House of Commons such as abortion and genetic engineering – topics about which MPs are often afraid of exposing their personal opinions in case it creates conflict with their constituents and parties.

On a daily basis, peers keep a close eye on the government by asking oral and written questions, responding to government statements or debating key issues. In all cases, the government's reply is a matter of public record, meaning that the House of Lords is able to make a significant contribution to improving transparency and the public's understanding of the government's actions.

Questions

Members can ask oral questions on any aspect of the government's activities in the chamber; these are answered by a government minister. While most questions are published in advance, the House has a separate procedure for tabling urgent 'private notice' questions. There is also the opportunity for written questions; these are used more often, and increasingly by members to extract information from the government.

Statements

The government often makes important announcements by means of an oral or written statement to one or both houses of parliament. Following an oral statement to the House of

Lords, members are able to question the government minister in order to raise concerns or seek clarification on any point of policy or fact.

Debates

Debates account for 30 per cent of business in the House of Lords chamber, with members not restricted to debating the legislative programme. They can propose debates on any topic, at the end of which a government minister responds to the questions, concerns and other matters that have been raised.

The professional expertise and specialist knowledge of members are valuable and help to ensure that issues and questions that otherwise might not be highlighted are brought to the government's attention. Because of this, debates in the House of Lords are effective in influencing the decision-making process and helping to shape policy and laws. This expertise was illustrated in a recent House of Lords debate on prescription charges in England that included former deans of university medical schools, dentists, former GPs, former consultants, professors of nursing, the president of Mencap and the former director of Age Concern (now Age UK).

Committees in the House of Lords have a different function from those in the Commons. Each Lords committee focuses on a broad subject area rather than a particular government department. The specialist knowledge and wide range of experience also allows for a more rigorous and independent approach to scrutiny.

Show your understanding

1 Explain, in detail, why some consider the Lords an effective scrutiniser of government policy.
2 Create a spider diagram detailing some of the key features of the House of Lords.
3 What part does the House of Lords play in the passing of legislation?

The Executive

The UK Executive is made up of three parts as follows:

- the prime minister
- the cabinet
- the civil service.

The Executive is the key decision-making body in the UK. It has the power, authority and legitimacy to make most of the decisions that affect all of our lives and is the main influence of the direction a country takes. This is primarily done through formulating and implementing policy. The prime minister and the cabinet are politically motivated and **partisan** in their decision-making capacity – together they make up the government. The civil service is politically neutral and it is their job to advise the government and carry out their plans.

> **Partisan** – devoted to the ideology or agendas of a political party.

Role of the prime minister

According to the prime minister's own website, the prime minister is head of the UK government and is ultimately responsible for the policy and decisions of the government. The key roles are overseeing the operation of the civil service, appointing members of the cabinet/government and being the principal government figure in the House of Commons.

A common misunderstanding relates to how the prime minister is selected. Unlike the president of the USA, the prime minister is not directly elected. In fact, the prime minister is chosen by the monarch, who through constitutional convention picks the person who has the support of the House of Commons; this is usually the leader of the largest political party in the

Commons. It is this majority that allows the prime minister to take the lead in government. The ultimate 'check' on the power of government and the prime minister lies with ordinary MPs. If a prime minster does not have the support of the majority of the House of Commons chamber, the Commons can pass a vote of no confidence, leading to the resignation of the prime minister and the government. This happened to the minority Labour government of James Callaghan in 1979. In the election that followed, the Conservatives, under Margaret Thatcher, came to power. Labour did not form a government again until 1997, when Tony Blair won with a landslide victory. More recently, in 2019, there was an unsuccessful vote of no confidence tabled against Theresa May. Many would argue that while it did not trigger a general election, it caused great political damage to May and contributed hugely to her eventual resignation.

Powers of the prime minister

With the role of the prime minister comes several powers that are given in order for them to be able to lead effectively. However, some of these powers vary depending upon a number of circumstances, many of which are out of the control of the prime minister. This was summed up by former prime minister Harold Macmillan; when asked by a journalist what he most feared he replied 'events, dear boy, events'. Given the COVID-19 outbreak in 2020, Boris Johnson may agree.

Royal prerogative

The prime minister holds prerogative powers. These are powers that were previously used by the monarch but are now used by the prime minister. They enable the leader to rule virtually by decree, without the backing of or consultation with parliament.

Some of these powers include:

- the recognition of foreign states
- the declaration of war
- the deployment of armed forces in the UK and abroad
- the making of treaties
- the accreditation of diplomats
- the appointment and dismissal of ministers
- the restructuring of government departments
- the appointment of special advisers
- the issuing and withdrawal of passports
- the granting of honours
- appointments to, and employment conditions of, the civil service
- the calling of elections.*

*limited by fixed-term parliaments

On an individual basis the majority of these powers are administrative but as a collective they make the prime minister the most powerful individual in office.

Show your understanding

1 Describe how a prime minister is selected.
2 Explain what happens to the prime minister in a 'vote of no confidence'.
3 Outline some of the prerogative powers exercised by the prime minister.

Sources and limitations of power

As well as the prerogative powers given to the prime minister, their position within parliament gives them a number of additional powers. What is significant about these extra powers is that they are subject to change. When describing the role of government the famous saying 'a week is a long time in politics' is used regularly and with regard to the amount of power a prime minister can yield it is particularly pertinent.

Majority party leadership

As the leader of the largest party in the House of Commons, the prime minister usually has a majority and therefore is able to implement the proposed government legislation; however, this varies depending on general election results. The Labour leader Tony Blair commanded great power and authority in his first two terms in office from 1997 to 2005, but this ebbed away from 2005 to 2007, when he left office earlier than intended. In his first term, from 2010 to 2015, Conservative leader David Cameron had to form a coalition with the Liberal Democrats to establish a Commons majority but lost the support of some MPs because of the compromises he made. In his most recent term he commanded a slim majority in the Commons; however, this meant that he was at risk of losing power if a small number of Conservative MPs defied the whip. Indeed it was widely rumoured that Cameron allowed the EU Referendum to take place due to pressure from a fairly small group of Conservative MPs, showing that his power was limited. More recently, Theresa May became prime minister in 2017 and enjoyed a slim majority initially. Following the 2017 general election she lost this advantage, formed a minority government and had to broker a deal with the DUP. When Boris Johnson became prime minister in 2019 he inherited this minority, but then won a large majority in the 2019 general election, giving him more power.

Image and popularity

A key source of prime ministerial power is their popularity among the general public. Prime ministers attract significant media attention and live with a high degree of public scrutiny as spokesperson for the government. They also provide national leadership both at home and on the international stage, leading the nation in times of crisis and emergency. They sit down with other world leaders and attend high-profile meetings, such as at the G8 and EU summits. They are directly involved in foreign policy, and it is the prime minister who negotiates treaties. A popular and well-liked prime minister will have the support of the people and this will be reflected in high ratings in the polls. David Cameron consistently had higher approval ratings than other high-profile Conservatives and opposition leaders, especially when it came to people's perception of him as an effective leader. The popularity of the leader directly affects the popularity of the party and so MPs will support a leader who is seen as an electoral asset because they bring with them a better chance of MPs retaining their status in future elections.

High-profile colleagues

In theory, the prime minister has the ability to create a cabinet in their own image. In reality, a prime minister's power within the cabinet is limited by a need to satisfy the ambitions of party colleagues. Senior party members and those who have been loyal and show potential may expect to be included in the government regardless of their own personal political views. The prime minister is also restricted by the pool of MPs that is available; while it is their only resource, it can also provide obstacles. The prime minister may be pushed into offering positions to potential rivals and opponents: these people may be less trouble inside the cabinet, where they are bound by the convention of collective responsibility, rather than outside it on the back benches, where they could stir up dissent and be a focus for rebels should a policy be controversial.

Margaret Thatcher, Conservative prime minister from 1979 to 1990, was regarded as a strong and effective leader. Yet 'the Iron Lady', as she was known, was effectively forced out of office by her cabinet colleagues in November 1990, thus demonstrating the limitations of the office of prime minister. Tony Blair was regarded as an effective leader, winning three elections in a row.

Prime Minister David Cameron had trouble with a section of his party who were more right-wing in their outlook, believing in reducing the role of state intervention. This was because of his support for giving some prisoners the vote, his home secretary's liberal views on law and order, and the cuts to the defence budget while the international aid budget was maintained. In fact, Cameron saw more of his own MPs rebel and faced more revolts in his first year in office than Tony Blair did during the whole of his first term.

Cameron made high-profile Conservative Boris Johnson a part-time member of the cabinet, because of his power in the party and his former role as mayor of London. Prime Minister Theresa May appointed Johnson as foreign secretary in her first cabinet in an attempt to prevent a split in the party, especially over the withdrawal from the EU. May was ultimately unsuccessful in keeping this influential group of Conservative MPs at bay and was eventually forced out as leader of the party to make way for Johnson in 2019. Johnson immediately included influential like-minded colleagues such as Michael Gove and Priti Patel in his cabinet.

Events

Several key events limited Gordon Brown's power as prime minister and eventually led to his defeat at the polls in 2010. For example, the global financial crisis, the unexpected backlash over the Gurkha resettlement issue and the damaging MPs' expenses controversies, followed by the resignations of several key cabinet members, were just some of the events during his premiership that indicated his dwindling power and support. Under Cameron's leadership a few events such as the migrant crisis and the independence and European referenda had a draining effect on his premiership and he effectively resigned from office after the June 2016 EU 'Leave' result. May's reign was dominated by negotiations with the EU. Johnson's leadership initially was dominated by controversy due to him proroguing parliament and also calling a general election. In early 2020, the COVID-19 crisis dominated the agenda for his government with the introduction of a number of financial aid packages to try and prevent catastrophic damage to the UK economy.

The opposition

The 'official opposition' is the largest minority party, and its main purpose is to oppose the government of the day. This can be both a source of and a drain on prime ministerial power. As leader of the largest opposition party (Labour), Sir Keir Starmer was elected in 2020 as opposition leader in the Commons. The leader of the opposition picks a shadow cabinet to follow and scrutinise the work of each government department and the policies being developed in their specific areas. A weak opposition leader can help elevate the prime minster, making them look even more statesman-like; however, a strong opposition leader can weaken the image of the prime minister.

Power of patronage

The prime minister also has the power to be involved in appointing people to important positions outside the government. For example, they can make political nominations to the House of Lords and are allowed to approve one person for a top ecclesiastical appointment in the Church of England. They also have the key role in the 'new year's honours list' in which the monarch awards people for their service to Britain through knighthoods, MBEs and CBEs.

The annual honours list always creates some controversy. Boris Johnson proposed a number of people for peerages in his first honours list. Many, such as Kenneth Clarke who had recently retired as an MP following decades in office, would be widely accepted; however, at times, party donors and close acquaintances are nominated and this can attract criticism. A committee assesses the merits of the prime minister's list and has to approve nominations.

Show your understanding

1. Explain the importance of a parliamentary majority for the prime minister.
2. What evidence is there to suggest that 'image' is important for the prime minister?
3. Explain why having high-profile colleagues can be both advantageous and damaging to prime ministerial power.
4. Describe some of the controversies surrounding the power of patronage.
5. 'A week is a long time in politics.' To what extent may this be true in relation to prime ministerial power?

Recent prime ministers

Tony Blair (1997–2007)

Tony Blair led the Labour Party to a landslide victory in 1997 and 2001, giving him huge power and achieving super majorities on both occasions. He had a celebrity-like status and was often courted by the media. Famously he hosted events in Downing Street to which he invited popular actors and musicians, which enhanced his image. In addition he featured as a special guest on TV shows such as the comedy programme *The Catherine Tate Show* as part of a Comic Relief Special. However, he only managed a much reduced majority in 2005 as his popularity began to dwindle, due primarily to his government's decision to invade Iraq and the subsequent failure to find any weapons of mass destruction, which had been their justification for entering the conflict. Tony Blair was seen as the first prime minister to take on a presidential style of leadership due to the importance placed on his image and his micromanagement style.

Gordon Brown (2007–10)

Gordon Brown began his premiership with a huge disadvantage, in that he had not led the party to success in a general election. Despite dealing decisively with the banking crisis of 2008 and 2009 and being a leading voice in the G20 summit on the issue, domestically he did not receive the credit he perhaps deserved. He failed to ever have the legitimacy of the office and also came up against a charismatic opposition leader in Cameron, which further damaged his image and popularity. Brown was widely disliked and lampooned at the hands of the media. His perceived lack of charisma and personality resulted in his ratings plummeting throughout 2009 and up to the election in 2010, and this resulted in a lack of support from some Labour MPs who felt he damaged their own chances of re-election.

David Cameron (2010–16)

Cameron was dealt an unusual hand in his first term in that he was the prime minister of a coalition government. This constrained his power in several ways. He always had to consult Deputy Prime Minister Nick Clegg on the direction of government, he had Liberal Democrat members in his cabinet and also he had to manage disappointed members of his own party who did not want to concede points to their coalition colleagues. Cameron was able to successfully navigate this difficult task due to his background in public relations and his role as facilitator. Following a majority win in 2015 he maintained this approach but had to concede his power slightly after he announced that he would not stand for a third term in 2020. Immediately after the 'Leave' victory in the EU Referendum, he announced that he would resign as prime minister following the appointment of a new leader of the Conservative Party. He therefore resigned on 13 July 2016 and Theresa May became the new Conservative leader and the new prime minister.

Theresa May (2016–19)

Theresa May became only the second female British prime minister in history and began decisively by sacking George Osborne from the chancellor of the exchequer position. She also dismissed Michael Gove from the position of justice minister.

She tried to build consensus in a divided Conservative Party but was unsuccessful. Her time in office was dominated by Britain's exit from the EU and, having voted for 'Remain' in the referendum, she was unable to control the increasingly influential 'Leave' camp within the party. While she fought and won a general election, the Conservative majority dissipated and as a result there was a hung parliament, which forced May into relying on the DUP for support in getting bills passed. At times, she was unfairly portrayed by the media as being 'awkward' in public. She was heavily criticised by many for her slow response to the Grenfell Tower fire, in which 72 people perished in June 2017. She did enjoy dominance over the leader of the opposition, Jeremy Corbyn, and developed a reputation for a strong performance during PMQs. She resigned in July 2019.

Figure 7.6 Theresa May

Boris Johnson (2019–?)

Boris Johnson replaced May as Conservative leader and therefore became the prime minister on 24 July 2019. Previously he had been a leading member of the Vote Leave campaign team and following his appointment he brought in other members of the 'Leave' team such as Michael Gove. He had inherited Theresa May's minority government and immediately came up against a resistant parliament. He found that he could not progress with his Brexit plans and as a result he controversially 'prorogued' (shut down) parliament in an attempt to force through legislation. In response, the Supreme Court ruled this unlawful and forced parliament to resume. During these Brexit debates 21 Conservative MPs, including Tory heavyweight Kenneth Clark, voted against the government and were suspended from the party. Johnson continued in this combative vein in order to progress with Brexit and called a general election to take place on 12 December. He led his party to a huge majority, which gave him the power to put his Brexit plans into place. His premiership would quickly become dominated by the COVID-19 outbreak, during which he

⇨

became infected with COVID-19 and spent two nights in intensive care on a ventilator. He made a full recovery. Since that event Johnson has repeatedly emphasised his personal fitness as being a contributor to his poor health when infected with COVID-19. He has attempted to rectify this by hiring a personal trainer, losing weight and promoting tackling obesity as a government priority.

Figure 7.7 Boris Johnson addressing the nation during the COVID-19 outbreak

Table 7.3 Five prime ministers compared

	Blair	Brown	Cameron	May	Johnson
Strategy	Directive	Indecisive	Facilitator	Consensus	Directive
Tactics	PM's office the centre of power	A limited return to the cabinet being the centre of power	Stable, managerial, careful coalition management	Managerial, reactive, heal divisions	Hardline approach to Brexit, PM office the centre of power
Context	Large majority, weak opposition, strong economy	Economic crisis, weak party, opposition renewal	Coalition government, deficit reduction, weak majority, migrant crisis and Europe	Brexit management, deficit, minority government	Huge conflict with parliament, Brexit hardline approach, COVID-19

Source: Politics Review

Power of appointment/dismissal

The power to appoint and dismiss government ministers – especially cabinet ministers – is arguably where most of the prime minister's regular power lies. It is the prime minister who decides which MPs to reward or punish by appointing them to specific posts and including them in or excluding them from the cabinet. This power to 'hire or fire' includes the power to 'reshuffle' (or refresh) the make-up of the cabinet or government whenever they deem it necessary. This can allow the prime minister to create a cabinet of loyal supporters; however, in reality it is best to consider the selection carefully, paying close attention to people's ambitions. If someone is overlooked for promotion they can become resentful, and it is important for the prime minister to retain the support and loyalty of all their MPs. In his memoirs Tony Blair calls those left out as the 'ejected, dejected and rejected' who eventually come to 'resent you' (Tony Blair, *A Journey*, 2010, Hutchinson).

Blair was forced to include Gordon Brown in the cabinet as chancellor of the exchequer from 1997 until his own resignation in 2007, and was effectively powerless to remove him due to a large section of the Labour Party being loyal to Brown. However, Blair used this to his tactical advantage so that publicly any disagreements between the pair were kept out of the public eye.

Cameron in his role as prime minister of a coalition government conceded some of this power to the deputy prime minister and Liberal Democrat leader Nick Clegg. Clegg had sole charge over the appointments of Liberal Democrat ministers. Political rival Boris Johnson was given a special invitation to the 'political cabinet', meaning that he would attend some cabinet meetings but not take a direct part in decision making. Many saw this as an attempt by Cameron to keep Johnson's backbench supporters under his control.

Cabinet chairperson

The prime minister chairs cabinet meetings, and in so doing has the power to set the agenda and determine what is discussed and – in some cases more importantly – what is not discussed. They also control the pace and direction of the meetings and sum up the 'sense' of what took place.

Under Tony Blair the cabinet met infrequently. Cabinet meetings tended to be short and informal gatherings to discuss the business of the day, involving round-the-table stock-take reports from the various government departments, which lasted no more than 40 minutes.

Under Cameron, cabinet government rose in importance because of the need for co-operation and consultation to make the coalition work. However, this arrangement put the convention

of collective responsibility under strain as government members were forced to support policies in public that they had opposed in their manifestos. More recently, the cabinet under May was assembled with Brexit in mind and included MPs on both sides of the Leave/Remain divide. However, May had chosen not to include key Brexiteers such as Michael Gove.

Under Johnson it would appear that the cabinet has a number of influential ministers such as Priti Patel and Dominic Raab. However, questions were asked about the role of the prime minister's special adviser Dominic Cummings and many feel that the balance of power is with the prime minister rather than shared among the cabinet.

Show your understanding

1 Create detailed profiles on each of the last three prime ministers.
2 Explain why being cabinet chairperson enhances the prime minister's power.

12-mark question

Analyse the powers of the prime minister.

The cabinet

The cabinet is essentially a government committee that is chaired by the prime minister. Every other member is in charge of a government department and with this position a minister is given the title of secretary of state, a large pay increase and huge influence over the way that the country is run. It is often seen as the pinnacle of a career in UK politics and these positions are coveted by ambitious MPs. The cabinet meets once per week to discuss the key events that are taking place in the governance of these departments. The cabinet is usually made up of between 20 and 25 ministers but this is at the discretion of the prime minister and they have full power over the appointments to these posts.

This group of MPs is the public face of government and so it is important that ministers support its collective decisions. It is a case of 'united we stand, divided we fall': a divided cabinet is a serious bleeding of prime ministerial power. The table in the cabinet room is deliberately oval-shaped so that the prime minister, who sits in the centre of one of the long sides, can see the faces and body language of all the Cabinet and so spot any small signs of loyalty or dissent.

The prime minister has traditionally been referred to as *primus inter pares*, which means 'first among equals', and demonstrates that they are a member of the collective decision-making body of the cabinet, rather than an individual who has powers in their own right. The prime minister is first among equals simply in recognition of the responsibility held for appointing and dismissing all the other cabinet members. This can make ministers feel that they are beholden to the prime minister and owe the prime minister their loyalty.

The prime minister chairs the meeting and sets its agenda; they also decide who speaks around the cabinet table and sum up at the end of each item. It is this summing up that becomes government policy, with all members being collectively responsible for all decisions and policies. The secretary of the cabinet is responsible for preparing records of its discussions and decisions. As the complexity of government decision making has evolved, more agents have become involved. Prime ministers are now more likely to consult with external think-tanks, cabinet committees and special advisers before making decisions. For example, COBRA (the Civil Contingencies Committee,

named after Cabinet Office Briefing Room A), which can be made up of both ministers and non-government officials, takes decisions on national security in emergency situations. This leads to the perception that the cabinet may be less important than it once was, and is only there to rubber-stamp decisions that have already been made or to present government policy and decisions.

Collective responsibility

Collective responsibility is at the heart of cabinet government. The cabinet tries to reach decisions on the basis that, as members of the government, ministers are collectively responsible and have to publicly support and defend those decisions regardless of their personal opinions – or resign. This again gives the prime minister great power as any cabinet disagreements are usually kept in-house and are not made public. However, when a cabinet minister does resign over a disagreement with government policy it can be hugely embarrassing for the prime minister. In February 2020 Boris Johnson was in the process of reshuffling his cabinet. Although he wanted to keep the chancellor of the exchequer, Sajid Javid, the minister resigned over changes that Johnson made to the chancellor's background staff. Publicly Javid continued to fully support Johnson, but the episode was awkward for the prime minister.

In recent governments, the division within the Conservative party over the exit from the EU has resulted in a number of cabinet reshuffles.

Show your understanding

1. Describe the main features of the cabinet.
2. Explain in detail the terms *'primus inter pares'* and *'collective responsibility'*.

The civil service

The civil service helps the government of the day to develop and deliver its policies as effectively as possible. The role of the senior civil service is to offer impartial advice to ministers and inform them of the possible consequences and the potential advantages and disadvantages of their actions or decisions. Civil servants are permanent in the sense that their appointment means they cannot be removed by a dissatisfied minister or following a general election. This continuity of tenure allows them to build up experience and expertise that is usually lacking in a minister, and enables them to offer genuinely neutral advice without the worry of any personal political implications. It also means that, because of the high turnover of government ministers, they are likely to serve many ministers. It has been calculated that the average tenure of a government minister in the Blair government was just 1.3 years, with junior ministers being moved more or less on an annual basis.

Many commentators would argue that civil servants are essential for an effective government as they are neutral. This means the advice they give to cabinet secretaries must be free from any bias towards the fortunes of one political party and must not be influenced by any political ideology.

Case study: Sir Philip Rutnam

The Home Office's top civil servant, Sir Philip Rutnam, resigned in February 2020 and announced plans to sue the government for constructive dismissal after a series of clashes with the home secretary, Priti Patel.

He stepped down after 33 years because he said he had become the 'target of vicious and orchestrated campaign against him', which he accused Patel of orchestrating.

Following his resignation there were a number of accusations of intimidation and bullying of civil servants by ministers and special advisers, which brought into sharp focus the relationship between civil servants and governments.

Special advisers

A special adviser or 'spad' is a minister's principal political confidant, advising, liaising and most famously spinning the party view. When you read comments by an 'aide' to a minister or 'sources close to the minister' in a newspaper, that's usually the spad commenting.

Spads hold a privileged and special role in government. Like civil servants, they are paid by the taxpayer but they do not need to be politically neutral. Whereas civil servants offer neutral advice to ministers, spads offer political advice. Their key purpose has been described as 'devilling' or 'squirrelling' away at all government policy and communications to ensure that it complies with or 'toes' the appropriate party or political line. Whereas civil servants must not engage in any political activity that could be interpreted as compromising their independence and must promise to act impartially, spads are openly political but cannot override advice from officials that they find unpalatable.

With the exception of the prime minister and their deputy, cabinet ministers generally have just two spads each. Former Prime Minister David Cameron approved the appointment of every special adviser. In his autobiography, Tony

Blair admits to having accumulated 70 at one point, which some considered excessive. However, he saw them as essential to speeding up the process of political decision making and a sensible way of enlarging the scope of available advice. This famously is referred to as Blair's 'sofa government', in reference to a string of accusations to the effect that he made many important decisions with his backroom team as opposed to his cabinet colleagues.

Unlike the appointment of civil servants, there is no merit-based process to the appointment of the spad. Ministers simply choose whoever they decide is best for the job; the only restriction is that the prime minister must approve every appointment.

Many feel as though spads have too much political influence on ministers. For example, there was concern over the influence that spad Dominic Cummings had on former education secretary, Michael Gove, over educational reforms that were seen as too radical by some. David Cameron's appointment of Christopher Lockwood to his team of advisers was seen as an example of cronyism and creating an 'inner political circle', which is not conducive to open government.

Boris backs his main adviser

In May 2020, during the COVID-19 outbreak, the prime minister's chief adviser Dominic Cummings was caught up in a scandal after it was revealed that he had travelled for hours to a family home to self-isolate after he suspected he was infected with COVID-19. This appeared to be in contrast to the government advice of 'Stay at Home'. In normal circumstances, an adviser who is unelected would probably have been sacked for damaging the government's key message; however, Dominic Cummings kept his job. Indeed, in an unprecedented move, Cummings gave a live statement to the media at 10 Downing Street, thrusting him into the limelight. Normally special advisers work behind the scenes. This highlighted Cummings' importance to the Johnson government, and indeed many suspect that Cummings wielded huge influence throughout the government, which brings into sharp focus the debate about how influential these advisers can be, despite having little accountability to the public. Cummings also sat on the Scientific Advisory Group for Emergencies, which produced the scientific evidence that was used to make plans for tackling COVID-19, such as the lockdown procedures he was accused of breaking. Cummings was later dismissed by Johnson in November 2020.

Conflict between spads and civil servants

In September 2001 Jo Moore, the spin doctor of Stephen Byers, minister for the Department of Transport, Local Government and the Regions (DTLR), had faced calls for her resignation when it became known that she had advised 'burying bad news' by issuing departmental press releases immediately after the 9/11 terrorist attacks.

Byers protected her, but Moore was forced to offer a public apology for her behaviour. Relations between Moore and the senior civil servants within the department, including the director of communications, Martin Sixsmith, were strained and hostile. In February 2002, more allegations against Jo Moore were leaked and she agreed to resign after Byers promised that Sixsmith would also be forced to resign.

Byers informed the House of Commons that he had accepted Sixsmith's resignation. This was untrue because Sixsmith had not offered his resignation. Byers was forced to resign because he had told the House a direct lie. As the *Sunday Times* stated, the whole affair highlighted 'a ministry in chaos and a government staffed by apparatchiks who had lost contact with the truth'.

In 2020, there were claims that Boris Johnson's senior special adviser, Dominic Cummings, was planning a reform of the way the civil service is run.

Show your understanding

1 Describe in detail the role of the civil service.
2 Outline the key criticisms of the civil service.
3 'The civil service has power without accountability.' To what extent is this statement accurate?
4 Describe in detail the role of special advisers.
5 Explain why many political commentators criticise the role of special advisers.

20-mark questions

1 To what extent can parliament effectively scrutinise the work of the Executive?
2 'The powers of the prime minister are limited by parliament and the Cabinet.' Discuss.

The Judiciary

Parliament is sovereign. It is the chief legislative body and is where the major decisions about the UK are made. In contrast to the USA, where the courts can strike down laws that are deemed to be unconstitutional, the UK's courts can only dream of such power as the UK has an uncodified constitution (see Chapter 1, page 2).

Arguments for court interference

The courts only have the power to rule on laws passed by parliament and often only on individual cases that the judges may see as being unlawful; however, the government can overrule the Judiciary through an Act of Parliament.

Many argue that the Judiciary plays an important role in the running of the country as it has huge experience, is unbiased and need only focus on enforcing the law fairly.

Arguments against court interference

The key argument against judges interfering in governance is that this would undermine the sovereignty of parliament. After all, MPs who create and process new laws through parliament are elected representatives and so have legitimacy to make laws that affect all citizens. Judges are unelected and often come from an elite middle-class background. This leaves them open to accusations of being out of touch with the issues that affect the lives of many ordinary citizens.

What is a pressure group?

A pressure group usually takes the form of an organisation of like-minded people who want to influence decision makers such as the government and other large organisations. Pressure groups aim to influence decision makers by drawing attention to specific issues or specific groups of people. They hope to put pressure on organisations and the government to change their behaviour. In particular, they hope to influence governments when it comes to the formation of legislation, the passing of bills and the amendment of existing laws. Pressure groups feel that they will have more success in pressuring the government as a group rather than as individuals. These groups can vary in size from a small group of locals protesting about changes to their local area to multinational organisations protesting about global issues.

Why do people join a pressure group?

Pressure groups do not usually want to be in government or in mainstream politics as they only have an interest in a particular issue or a particular group of people. For some the traditional method of participating in democracy through political parties is not an attractive prospect. They feel that party politics is perhaps too wide a focus and would rather be involved with an organisation that offers a narrower and more specific focus, usually on a single issue that can seem more important and more appealing to many. As a result we have seen in recent decades a movement away from political party membership towards pressure group membership.

While there has recently been an upsurge in membership of the Labour Party in the UK, since the 1960s membership of political parties has declined. Many commentators have suggested that public lack of interest in mainstream politics is the main reason for this. An overall lack of trust in politicians and in mainstream politics itself has resulted in some people looking towards pressure groups as a more honest and accessible way to become involved in politics.

What are the aims of pressure groups?

The role of pressure groups in influencing the decision-making process of a democratic system is a hotly debated subject. While some argue that they enhance the democratic process, others argue that they threaten democracy. Part of this debate relates closely to the aims of pressure groups. Many pressure groups have a specific set of aims. Indeed, there are thousands of short-life pressure groups, which are usually locally organised and look to influence decision makers about an issue that affects local communities. For example, in April 2019, a group from Bo'ness Road Action Group (BRAG) held a public rally to protest at the plans of INEOS (a Grangemouth petrochemical plant's owners) to close a road in the area that was used by locals.

BRAG

The Bo'ness Road Action Group (BRAG) was set up in 2018 by local residents of Bo'ness and Grangemouth over plans to close a road in Grangemouth near the petrochemical plant owned by INEOS. They argued that closing the road would be harmful to the local economy. They also complained that, despite Falkirk Council initially denying planning permission, the Scottish government had overruled the decision and that this was damaging to local democracy in Scotland. Ultimately the group were unsuccessful but they gained support from the community with their presence in local newspapers, local rallies and petitions.

However, other pressure groups have aims that will not be met in the short term. These groups tend to be more disruptive in their methods and at times their aims will conflict with the democratic process. For example, in April 2019, a large protest by Extinction Rebellion took place in London and other cities in the UK. They were protesting about climate change and a lack of investment by governments. While many would sympathise with their cause, they will be unlikely to succeed in the short term with their aims. This can lead to frustration and in some instances violence.

Figure 8.1 Extinction Rebellion

Extinction Rebellion

In April 2019 a group of climate protestors called Extinction Rebellion brought parts of London to a standstill over a ten-day period. They were protesting against the UK government and its institutions' approach to climate change, which they feel is too slow. They want the government to declare a national emergency and radically change their policies. During the protest, they closed roads at a number of busy London junctions such as Marble Arch. They also attempted to disrupt railways, Underground stations and airports and even glued themselves to the entrance of the London Stock Exchange. Due to their illegal actions, it was always highly unlikely that the government would change their policies; the protest did, however, gain a lot of publicity for climate-change issues.

Show your understanding

1 Describe some of the key features of a pressure group.
2 Explain, with examples, three reasons why someone would become a member of a pressure group.
3 Explain the link between pressure group aims and likely success.

Cause groups

Members of cause groups usually have a shared belief or view, so groups are set up to promote a specific cause in which members have an interest. A key feature of cause groups is that anyone can become a member. As long as you have an interest in the cause, you can participate fully in its operations. Cause groups can be in existence for a short period or over the longer term. For example, We Like Milngavie was a cause group set up with the aim of preventing a huge expansion of a Tesco supermarket in the area. It was a temporary group and campaigned while this was an issue, but disbanded after Tesco announced that they were dropping the planned expansion of their store. On the other hand, a cause group such as Age UK, which aims to promote the rights of elderly citizens, has been around for a much longer period.

Sectional groups

Sectional groups are set up to represent and promote the material interests of a specific group of people in society. These groups will be interested in the needs of their members only. The most popular form of sectional group is a trade union, which looks after the interests of workers. For example, the Scottish Secondary Teachers' Association is a trade union that only represents secondary teachers in Scotland and has no interest in promoting any other groups. Only Scottish secondary school teachers can be members and so it is not open to all.

Insider or outsider?

As well as being categorised by what they campaign for, pressure groups can also be classified by how they go about carrying out their campaigns. Pressure groups can elect to work with the government and hope to curry favour with decision makers; these groups are known as insider groups. However, pressure groups may elect to work against the government and at times may be in conflict with decision makers; these groups are known as outsider groups. It should be noted that an insider group can become an outsider group, depending on which political party is in power. Trade unions are a perfect example of such a group. In the period from 1997 to 2010, trade unions were an insider group and played an important role in working with the Labour government to improve pay and working

conditions for ordinary workers. The introduction of the national minimum wage, EU working time directives and an expansion of tax credits for those in work all helped to reduce family and child poverty. However, since 2010 and under consecutive Conservative prime ministers, the power of trade unions to influence government policy has reduced substantially.

Insider groups

As mentioned, insider groups work with the government with the hope of persuading them to address the needs of their cause or members. For this arrangement to be successful, insider pressure groups will often need to carry out their campaigns in a professional and organised manner. They will likely campaign through organised meetings and events and may, in fact, 'have the ear' of the government as they are consulted by decision makers.

Insider groups normally represent professional bodies such as law and medicine. As a result they are often regarded as experts in their fields and can in fact be seen as key stakeholders in drafting legislation and so are part of the policy-formation process. In January 2019, the UK government completed a review of GPs and their future role in the NHS. Working with the British Medical Association (BMA), the review found that a substantial innovation in the use of digital technology in GP practices was needed. As a result, the UK government has looked into various technologies such as the use of Amazon's Alexa in partnership with the NHS. Many of these pressure groups are not well known to the general public as they often seek change 'behind closed doors' in areas that may not be seen as particularly newsworthy.

However, there are limits to the influence of an insider group on government decision making, especially if it disagrees with government policies. For example, the Conservative government wished to change the working conditions of all junior doctors in England and Wales in 2016, a move opposed by the BMA. With the government refusing to back down, doctors were forced to take strike action. This shows that the positions of trade unions can be variable. Traditionally, the BMA were considered an insider group but, in recent times, they have positioned themselves on the outside.

Figure 8.2 Trade unionists marching against a government bill

Outsider groups

Whereas some pressure groups may 'have the ear' of the government, many find themselves forced to challenge and at times disrupt the work of government. On many occasions these pressure groups act out in public to try to draw attention to their cause or issue. At times, this can even become destructive, chaotic and violent, resulting in law breaking and arrests. This means that they usually have a negative relationship with government and will be excluded from the policy-making process. It is this exclusion that can lead many groups to take direct action as they feel that their concerns are not being noted by decision makers and so they have to pressure them by bringing publicity to their issue. For example, in February 2018, a pressure group called Sisters Uncut stormed the BAFTA (British Academy of Film and Television Arts) awards ceremony in London in protest

against the UK government's domestic violence bill, which they felt would lead to women being arrested or detained. The group wore t-shirts with slogans and invaded the red carpet, raising huge publicity for their cause.

Owing to the very public nature of their protests, outsider pressure groups often have a much bigger public profile and are covered more prominently by the press.

Table 8.1 Insider and outsider pressure groups

Insiders	Outsiders
Are compatible with government	Are incompatible with government
Are regularly consulted by the decision makers	Are not regularly consulted
Work with the government	Engage in direct action and civil disobedience to put pressure on the decision makers
Have privileged status	Are not seen as having useful expertise or objectivity
Have expert knowledge	Usually campaign on controversial issues

Show your understanding

1 Describe, using examples, some of the key differences between cause and sectional groups.
2 Create a detailed table explaining the advantages and disadvantages of being an insider group and of being an outsider group.
3 In your own words, explain the terms 'ear of the government' and 'behind closed doors' in relation to pressure groups.
4 Why do you think that some groups feel the need to become an outsider group?
5 Why are trade unionists and the Scottish government against the 2016 Trade Union Bill?

Develop your skills

With a partner, create a detailed presentation on pressure groups with the aim of identifying cause, sectional, insider and outsider features. Use examples to justify your findings.

How influential are pressure groups?

A key debate regarding pressure groups is whether they are influential and/or successful in the UK's democratic system. While most would recognise that they can have influence in decision making, the extent of this influence is heavily dependent upon a number of factors:

- their relationship with the government of the day (as discussed earlier)
- the group's aims and context
- the group's status and access
- methods
- the group's resources.

Group aims and context

Precisely what a pressure group hopes to achieve is central to assessing their chances of influencing decision making. If their goal is seen as unachievable, open-ended, expensive or global then it becomes harder to recognise their success. For example, the Campaign for Nuclear Disarmament (CND) hopes not only to bring to an end the UK's nuclear deterrent but also to achieve a worldwide Nuclear Weapons Convention that would ban all nuclear weapons. The CND has been campaigning for a number of decades and is likely to continue to do so for decades to come. The CND may argue that it is successful for merely bringing the issue into the public's consciousness but it is unlikely to ever fully achieve its goals in an increasingly complex world.

However, smaller pressure groups with more achievable aims can be fully successful if they gain the change they seek. For example, Tripping Up Trump was a small-scale but influential pressure group that protested about the efforts of President Trump's company to expand his golf resort in the Menie Estate, Aberdeenshire. The group argued that the land deserved to be protected as it is of environmental importance. One way in which the group was successful was by acquiring land around the site, so restricting Trump's planned expansion.

In addition, groups whose aims enjoy a large measure of support among the broader public and legislators are more likely to be successful. These groups are 'pushing at an open door' and will fare better than those 'swimming against the tide' of public opinion. For example, Jamie Oliver's Feed Me Better campaign was always likely to receive more public backing than the National Association for the Care and Resettlement of Offenders' efforts to rehabilitate and resettle former prisoners.

Lastly, through time, various issues drift in and out of public debate and, if timed correctly, a pressure group can have great success. For example, in the early 1970s, environmental campaign groups such as Friends of the Earth would have struggled to gain influence. However, as the effects of global warming have become more apparent and the popularity of activists such as Greta Thunberg is raising the public's awareness of these issues, they may find that attitudes towards their aim are more positive and may result in more success.

Figure 8.3 Greta Thunberg

Group status and access

As mentioned previously, if a pressure group is regarded as an 'insider' group it is more likely to have its demands met by government. The Confederation of British Industry (CBI) is an organisation that represents the interests of thousands of businesses across the UK. It is often a key stakeholder in the formation of government policies relating to the business sector. Indeed, the group's close relationship with government was reflected during the COVID-19 outbreak. The CBI were consulted by the Treasury as they provided various measures to prevent small to medium-size businesses collapsing. One measure was accessibility to loans for companies that had to shut their operations down. The CBI's director general Carolyn Fairbairn commented some weeks later that the government had to make grants accessible for smaller firms who did not qualify for these loans.

Methods

The methods that a pressure group may use to promote its cause and/or issue can have a significant effect on its influence. If a pressure group feels that it has strong influence, it will probably be prepared to keep its actions low-key and more conventional; however, if a pressure group feels that it has little influence or that it is simply being ignored by decision makers then it may publicly protest in a legal manner – this is known as direct action. This will often set it on a collision course with the government. The more public a pressure group's methods are, the more likely it is to become an outsider group. Pressure groups need to have a cautious approach to protesting publicly. If they begin to be disruptive and break laws then they will be using illegal methods and as a result are highly unlikely to be successful.

Black Lives Matter

In May and June 2020, hundreds of thousands of people demonstrated across the UK in a show of solidarity against racism. The protest was organised under the banner of Black Lives Matter (BLM) and generated support in a number of smaller protests. These protests were restricted due to the COVID-19 pandemic, however their presence was felt in most major cities and towns across the UK. BLM is a political and social movement that protests against police brutality and racially motivated violence. Following the murder of George Floyd in Minneapolis in May 2020 there were global protests against institutional racism.

Show your understanding

1 Explain briefly the link between a group's aims and success.
2 Using examples, create a spider diagram showing the link between aims and success.
3 Explain the term 'stakeholder' in relation to pressure groups and influence.

Table 8.2 Pressure group methods

Conventional methods	
Petitions	These can be found via the government's official petitions website and other independent petition websites such as change.org and 38degrees.org.uk. Success stories have included the campaign to save BBC 6 Music radio station from closure and the Gurkha Justice Campaign.
Letter-writing campaigns	These are often used by human rights groups such as Amnesty International to put pressure on politicians. Their Write for Rights campaign encourages visitors to their website to write in support of individuals who have had their human rights infringed.
Marches	Well-organised and peaceful marches are often used to build public support. In October 2018 thousands of women marched to Parliament Square in London to protest against state pension inequality. WASPI (Women against State Pension Inequality) organised the march in protest against pension-age changes.
Lobbying	This involves setting up meetings to try to persuade politicians to join or support the group's cause. This method was used very successfully by the Gurkha Justice Campaign.
Research	Many groups commission studies and reports to help boost their cause. While not a pressure group, the Joseph Rowntree Foundation has commissioned many studies on poverty. Their annual report in February 2020 highlighted how the government must support people in the lowest-paid jobs to move into higher pay and access sufficient and secure working hours. They also stressed the need to strengthen our benefit system and increase the amount, quality and availability of low-cost housing. In addition, groups can develop this into a legal challenge. The Child Poverty Action Group has made numerous legal challenges to the government's welfare changes, including the controversial introduction of Universal Credit.
Direct action	
Legal stunts	Surfers Against Sewage have attracted media attention by posing for pictures wearing gas masks, and sitting on toilets on the beach.
Blockades/ occupying areas	In the early 2000s oil refineries were blockaded in protest at high fuel taxes, causing fuel shortages. The government has since been reluctant to increase tax on fuel. In May 2020, Extinction Rebellion closed off Trafalgar Square in London by placing over 2,000 pairs of children's shoes in rows to remind the UK government, during the COVID-19 outbreak, about the climate crisis and its long-term effect on children. In Scotland, the 'Bairns Not Bombs' protest in April 2015 blockaded the entrance to Faslane Naval Base near Helensburgh in an attempt to close down the base for the UK's nuclear deterrent. While illegal, the protest was successful in closing down the base for one day.
Toppling statues	In 2020, as part of the Black Lives Matter protests, demonstrators in Bristol pulled down the statue of Edward Colston, a seventeenth-century merchant and slave trader. After toppling the statue, the protestors threw it into Bristol harbour.
Illegal activity	Student protests against tuition fees in London in 2010 turned violent. Windows were smashed, Prince Charles' motorcade was attacked and more than 50 people were injured. In November 2015 the anti-capitalist Million Mask March organised by a group called Anonymous ended violently with more than 50 arrests for assaults on police officers, their horses and the destruction of a police car. In October 2019 over 1,100 activists were arrested in the London Extinction Rebellion protests.

Figure 8.4 'Bairns not Bombs' protest

Group resources

The human resources available to the group, such as the size of membership and the skills, can be key factors in determining success. In addition, the finances and equipment available to the group can have a huge effect on the impact it can make. Groups that benefit from a sizeable membership, such as the Royal Society for the Protection of Birds (RSPB) with more than 1.2 million members, are bound to receive more attention from decision makers and will likely also benefit from greater finances than those with smaller memberships, although increasingly smaller pressure groups are using 'crowdfunding' tools and websites to generate finances for campaigns. In addition, groups that possess necessary skills will have an advantage over others. For example, it is suggested that groups whose members are more financially and educationally privileged may have more chance of success as they are in a stronger position to articulate their aims.

In recent times celebrity endorsements have seemed to gain influence – not least as they attract coverage from the media. Emma Watson's work in promoting gender inequality for HeForShe and also Jamie Oliver's support of the Feed Me Better campaign, which helped to make changes to school food in England and Wales, have helped propel these groups into the limelight. As a result they are likely to gain the attention of decision makers.

Show your understanding

1. In your own words, explain why pressure groups choose a variety of methods to get their views heard.
2. Create a detailed spider diagram of the different methods used by pressure groups.
3. Choose two conventional methods and two direct actions and use the internet to find recent examples of each of these being used. Write a report on each example and how effective it was in achieving the group's aims.
4. Explain:
   a) why celebrity endorsements are an effective resource for pressure groups
   b) why a larger membership is likely to gain the attention of government
   c) the link between social class and pressure groups.

Digital democracy

A key feature of pressure group action in the twenty-first century is the growth of digital democracy. This use of technology in the democratic process has meant that many pressure groups are able to effectively use social media to spread influence. Digital democracy allows groups to mount campaigns and spread their influence, even if they have modest budgets and resources. It also enables people to become more easily involved in political action. Pressure groups can use digital democracy to educate but it also encourages people to express political views and even organise direct action. However, there has been some debate about how effective digital democracy is in influencing decision makers, and some accuse those who participate in social media campaigns of doing the bare minimum for a cause. In 2020, a number of movements used social media platforms such as Instagram to promote their causes and generate publicity. For example, the hashtag #rhodesmustfall was used in the campaign to have a statue of Cecil Rhodes removed from Oxford University due to his links with slavery in the eighteenth century.

Prominent pressure groups and other campaign organisations such as 38 Degrees can organise campaigns efficiently by using the internet. This can involve mass emailing campaigns, lobbying and letter-writing campaigns.

Social media has particularly enabled groups to organise direct action effectively. While outsider pressure groups have regularly used direct action, they now have the tools to organise protests and events at very short notice and with very little financial cost. This has sometimes led to civil disobedience and law breaking because the police have not been able to mobilise quickly enough in response. Pressure group UK Uncut has often used social media to organise events and protests; most famously members took over branches of Starbucks and food store Fortnum & Mason in London, turning them into services, such as nurseries and libraries, that they considered as being threatened by these companies' policies on paying tax.

38 Degrees

38 Degrees is a campaigning organisation with an online community of more than 2 million ordinary citizens. While not fighting for one particular issue, it backs campaigns that its community deems to be important and puts pressure on government and companies via petitions and various other campaign methods.

The name 38 Degrees comes from the angle at which human-caused avalanches are most likely to happen. According to 38 Degrees it gives individuals 'a chance to join an avalanche of people working together for a better world'. The group claims to have had significant influence – in 2013 it led a campaign against government plans to allow the use of pesticides that could harm bees. In April of that year the group delivered a petition of 280,000 signatures to Downing Street and thousands of supporters took part in the March of the Beekeepers on Parliament Square. Following this, major selling website eBay banned the selling of these pesticides.

In 2020 a campaign was launched on 38 Degrees to give support to the BBC following reports that the UK government was looking at the possibility of scrapping the TV licence. By May 2020 it had collected over 300,000 signatures and it helped more than 100,000 people take part in a key government consultation on the issue.

Figure 8.5 The junior doctors' protest in November 2015

Are pressure groups good for democracy?

Arguments for

Pressure groups are regarded by many as an important means of maintaining pluralism and thus improving democracy. Pluralism means exercising power in a variety of ways so it is dispersed as widely as possible so that all citizens can be seen as partners, and therefore share in the responsibility for the direction in which the nation is heading.

Dealing as they often do with minority and specialised issues, pressure groups are a vital link between the public and the government. They encourage people to participate in the democratic process regularly, not just every five years when casting votes in general elections. Also, pressure groups are much more accepted as a legitimate avenue for political participation by the general public than political parties. This is evident in the retaining and recruitment of members.

Pressure groups also play a critical role in publicising issues and in turn educating the public. They can influence public opinion and play a key role in getting all the 'facts out' for the public to scrutinise and then use to hold those with power to account. Pressure groups can help hold a government to account throughout their time in office by protesting about undesirable government policies, urging action on issues and

even enhancing 'traditional' politics by giving evidence to committees in parliament. It could also be argued that they offer a more 'honest' form of politics, which, unlike the party system, does not have to consider distracting influences such as career progression, political deals and control of media spin.

Arguments against

It could be argued, however, that any pressure on our elected representatives by external and minority interests threatens our whole democratic process. Inequalities also exist between pressure groups. Well-resourced, wealthy and middle-class pressure groups have a fast track to getting their views heard by those in power due to insider status. Increasingly, wealthy groups are hiring the services of specialist lobbying firms in an attempt to improve their chances of influencing those in power, adding weight to the argument that elitist sections of society wield excessive influence over government policies.

The methods that some pressure groups deploy can also challenge their role in a democracy. At times they can be extreme, violent and illegal. While many may argue that this is justified given our right to free speech, when pressure groups go to extremes it can actually result in people's right to free speech being limited by the authorities to ensure public safety. Also, pressure groups tend to focus on one issue to the exclusion of others. They represent only one side of an argument and challenge the government on that viewpoint, since the government has a responsibility to look at all aspects of an issue.

Lastly, in our system political parties are elected using democratic means. They have systems in place where they are elected to stand as candidates and then fight elections in a democratic way. However, pressure groups are not bound by any democratic rules. They are accountable only to their members and not a wider electorate. The organisation may not be internally democratic either and its actions may not necessarily reflect all of its members' views and wishes. The key argument is that pressure groups lack democratic legitimacy and so should not be imposing their will on a democratically elected government.

Case study: Liberty

Cause group Liberty works to protect basic rights and freedoms. It achieves this through a mixture of peaceful demonstrations, campaigns and legal action. Its former director is well-known human rights lawyer (and now member of the House of Lords) Shami Chakrabarti, who successfully led the group in challenging the New Labour government of 1997–2010 in their attempts to extend the 28 days' detention without charge for suspected terrorists to up to 90 days. Liberty argued that this went against human rights and threatened to challenge these plans through the courts. Liberty would argue that it enhances democracy as it represents disadvantaged groups against the might of powerful government and large corporations. However, it could also be argued that Liberty is one-sided and so has limited a democratically elected government's responsibility to ensure our safety.

Figure 8.6 Shami Chakrabarti

Show your understanding

1 Explain why pressure groups are seen as essential to maintaining democratic pluralism.
2 Read through the arguments for and against pressure groups being good for democracy.
   a) What do you consider are the strongest reasons for? Ensure you are detailed in your answer.
   b) Outline the key reasons that would be used to argue that pressure groups can damage democracy.

20-mark question

To what extent are pressure groups a threat to democracy? You should refer to Scotland or the UK or both in your answer.

Higher course assessment

The course assessment is made up of two components:

- two question papers with questions from each of the three sections and skills activities (80 marks)
- the Higher assignment (30 marks).

The marks awarded for the question papers and the assignment are added together and an overall mark indicates pass or fail. The course award is graded A to D.

Free-standing units at SCQF (Scottish Credit and Qualifications Framework) level 6

Students, who for whatever reason may not be proceeding to the exam itself, may be entered and assessed for the free-standing units in Democracy in Scotland and the UK, which no longer form part of the exam.

Outcome 1

Use between two and four sources of information to detect and explain the degree of objectivity in contexts relating to democracy in the Scottish and United Kingdom political systems.

Outcome 2

Draw on factual and theoretical knowledge and understanding of Scottish and United Kingdom political systems to give detailed description, explanations and analysis of a complex political issue.

The question papers

Question paper 1 has three sections:

- Section 1: Democracy in Scotland and the UK
  You will answer one essay from a choice of **three** (12 or 20 marks).
- Section 2: Social Issues in the UK
  You will answer one essay from a choice of **two** from your **chosen study** (12 or 20 marks).
- Section 3: International Issues
  You will answer one essay from a choice of **two** from your **chosen study** (12 or 20 marks).

You will have 1 hour and 45 minutes to answer the two 20-mark questions and one 12-mark question.

Question paper 2 has three mandatory questions as outlined below.

You will have 1 hour and 15 minutes to answer the two 10-mark questions and one 8-mark question.

What types of question will I need to answer in question paper 2?

There are three types of skills questions that you will have to practise in class. These are:

1 Using between two and four sources of information to **detect and explain the degree of objectivity** of a given statement (**10 marks**)
2 Using between two and four sources of information to **identify what conclusions can be drawn** (**10 marks**)
3 Using sources of information to **evaluate their reliability** (**8 marks**).

In the knowledge section of the exam you will answer four types of questions. Examples of the style of questions are given below.

Evaluate the effectiveness of parliamentary representatives in holding the government to account. (**12 marks**)

Analyse the potential impact of leaving the EU. (**12 marks**)

Analyse the influence of the media on voting behaviour. (**12 marks**)

To what extent are pressure groups effective in influencing government decisions? (**20 marks**)

Electoral systems do not always provide for fair representation. **Discuss.** (**20 marks**)

The assignment

The assignment is worth 30 marks out of a total of 110 marks for the course, and contributes 27 per cent of the total marks for the course. The assignment task is to research a Modern Studies issue with alternative views. You will use your two one-sided A4 sheets (Modern Studies research evidence) to support you in presenting the findings of your research. The duration of the write-up is 1 hour and 30 minutes.

The assignment applies research and decision-making skills in the context of a Modern Studies issue. You can choose a political, social or international issue. The information collected should display knowledge and understanding of the topic or issue chosen. SQA recommends that you should devote about 8 hours to the research stage, including preparation time for the production of evidence.

The results of the research will be written up under controlled assessment conditions and must be completed within 1 hour and 30 minutes. Your Modern Studies research evidence recorded on up to two single-sided sheets of A4 will consist of materials collected during the research stage of the assignment. As the SQA website shows, the allocation of marks is based on the following success criteria:

1 Identify and display knowledge and understanding of the issue about which a decision is to be made, including alternative courses of action

You should choose a decision about which there are alternative views, for example:

To recommend or reject the continuation of FPTP as the UK voting system

or

To recommend or reject the setting up of an elected UK second chamber

You should agree an issue to research with your teacher. Best practice is that your assignment should relate to one or more of the issues that you study in your course:

- Democracy in Scotland and the UK
- Social Issues in the UK
- International Issues.

> Be careful to ensure that your assignment is a Modern Studies issue and not one more relevant to RMPS (Religious, Moral and Philosophical Studies) or Environmental Science.

2 Analysing and synthesising information from a range of sources including use of specified resources

You will research a wide range of sources to widen your knowledge and understanding of the issue and to provide contrasting views on your chosen issue. By linking information from a variety of sources and viewpoints, you will be able to enrich and synthesise the arguments that are developed in your report. Remember it is important to provide balance in your report and to consider the arguments against your final decision/recommendation.

3 Evaluating the usefulness and reliability of a range of sources of information

You will comment on the background and nature of the source. Does it provide only one point of view? Are its findings up to date and so are its comments still relevant today?

4 Communicating information using the convention of a report

Remember you are *not* writing an essay. Your report style should include:

- a title
- a formal style that refers to evidence rather than personal opinion
- section headings breaking up the information to present evidence and contrasting arguments in a clear and logical structure
- references to the evidence you have used, especially the research evidence referred to in your A4 sheets
- a statement of the decision you have reached based on the evidence provided.

5 Reaching a decision, supported by evidence about the issue

Your decision should be based on your research evidence and your own background knowledge of the issue.

Possible Democracy titles for your assignment

- Should the House of Lords be replaced by an elected second chamber?
- Should a PR system be used to elect our MPs to the House of Commons?
- Should the United Kingdom introduce a written constitution?
- Should the voting age be reduced to 16 in UK elections?

Research methods

In Modern Studies we look at a range of political, social and international issues that affect everyone's lives. Many of these issues are based on evidence gathered through research carried out by a whole series of people and organisations – from the government to charities.

Figure 9.1 **Gathering evidence by research**

How do I carry out a piece of research?

When researching a topic in Modern Studies, it is important to consider where you will get your information from. In the twenty-first century, you have access to huge amounts of information on the internet. However, you need to be conscious of its accuracy and the likelihood of it containing bias and exaggeration.

Where do I gather information from?

The information gathered from research can be broken down into two parts: primary information and secondary information. Both provide qualitative and quantitative information.

Primary information

Primary information is evidence that you have gathered by yourself and that is unique to your personal research. The ways in which you gather primary evidence can vary greatly. Here are some examples:

- surveys/questionnaires
- interviews
- emails
- letters
- focus groups
- field studies.

Secondary information

Secondary information is evidence that you have gathered from research carried out by others. You should use it to help support your personal (primary) research. There are vast amounts of secondary information available. See the list on the next page for just some examples.

- books, newspapers and magazines
- official statistics
- internet search engines and websites
- television and radio programmes
- mobile phone apps
- social media such as Twitter
- library research.

Qualitative and quantitative research

Qualitative research is more focused on how people feel, what their thoughts are and why they make certain choices or decisions. Focus group meetings or one-to-one interviews are typical forms of qualitative research. Quantitative research largely uses methods such as questionnaires and surveys with set questions and tick-box answers. It can collate a large amount of data that can be analysed easily and used to formulate conclusions. Table 9.1 compares both types of research.

Table 9.1 **Qualitative and quantitative research**

	Qualitative research	**Quantitative research**
Objective/ purpose	To gain an understanding of underlying reasons and motivations To provide insights into the setting of a problem, generating ideas and/or hypotheses for later quantitative research To cover prevalent trends in thought and opinion	To quantify data and generalise results from a sample to the population of interest To measure the incidence of various views and opinions in a chosen sample Sometimes followed by qualitative research, which is used to explore some findings further
Sample	Usually a small number of non-representative cases. Respondents selected to fulfil a given quota	Usually a large number of cases representing the population of interest. Randomly selected respondents
Data collection	Unstructured or semi-structured techniques, e.g. individual depth interviews or group discussions	Structured techniques such as online questionnaires, or on-street or telephone interviews
Data analysis	Non-statistical	Statistical data is usually in the form of tabulations (tabs). Findings are conclusive and usually descriptive in nature
Outcome	Exploratory and/or investigative. Findings are not conclusive and cannot be used to make generalisations about the population of interest. They develop an initial understanding and sound base for further decision making	Used to recommend a final course of action

Source: www.snapsurveys.com/qualitative-quantitative-research

Acknowledgements

Figure 1.7 © Mirrorme22, Nilfanion, TUBS, Sting, CC BY-SA 3.0, https://commons.wikimedia.org/wiki/File:United_Kingdom_EU_referendum_2016_area_results_2-tone.svg; Extract in box 'Reaction in Scotland' used with permission of NFU Scotland, www.nfus.org.uk/news/news/food-and-farming-future-put-at-risk-by-migration-proposals; Extract from 'Hospitality is all about people … it just can't be automated' by Hannah Rodger and Tom Gordon, 20 February 2020, published in *The Herald*, used with permission; Extract from 'Immigration crackdown will create a "perfect storm" for Scotland' by Hannah Rodger, Tom Gordon and Alistair Grant, 20 February 2020, published in *The Herald*, used with permission; Content for the box 'UK points-based immigration system' and Table 1.4 taken from 'The UK's points-based immigration system: policy statement', 19 February 2020, www.gov.uk/government/publications/the-uks-points-based-immigration-system-policy-statement/the-uks-points-based-immigration-system-policy-statement; Iain MacWhirter (2014) *Disunited Kingdom: How Westminster Won a Referendum but Lost Scotland*, Cargo. ISBN 9781908885272; Official data collated by Our World in Data taken from https://ourworldindata.org/grapher/covid-vaccination-doses-per-capita?tab=chart&stackMode=absolute&time=latest&region=World under CC BY 4.0 https://creativecommons.org/licenses/by/4.0/deed.en_US; Definition of 'Sewel Convention' taken from www.parliament.uk/site-information/glossary/sewel-convention/; Extract from Nicola Sturgeon in the box 'No to devolved immigration' taken from 'Plan for Scottish visa: First Minister's speech', 27 January 2020, www.gov.scot/publications/plan-scottish-visa/; Content of the box 'The Sustainable Growth Commission Report, 2018' adapted from 'Scotland – The new case for optimism', The Sustainable Growth Commission, www.sustainablegrowthcommission.scot/report; The data in Table 3.7 is taken from 'The 2019 General Election: Voters Left Voiceless', 2 March 2020, Electoral Reform Society, www.electoral-reform.org.uk/latest-news-and-research/publications/the-2019-general-election-voters-left-voiceless/#sub-section-33; Extract from P.J. Pulzer taken from Peter Pulzer (1972) *Political Representation and Elections in Britain*, revised edn, London: Allen & Unwin, p. 102; Content in Fact file on 'Electoral turnout' taken from 'The 2015 General Election: A Voting System in Crisis', 26 July 2015, with permission of Electoral Reform Society, www.electoral-reform.org.uk/latest-news-and-research/publications/the-2015-general-election-report/; Extract from 'Jeremy Corbyn was "toxic" to voters says Scotland's last Labour MP Ian Murray' by Ian Murray, 13 December 2019, *Daily Record*, courtesy of Mirrorpix/Reach Licensing, www.dailyrecord.co.uk/news/politics/jeremy-corbyn-toxic-voters-says-21093775; Content in Table 4.8 used with permission of Opinium; Headline 'Your vote has never been more vital. Today, you MUST brave the deluge to go to your local polling station and back… BORIS', 12 December 2019, *Daily Mail*, used with permission of Daily Mail; Headline 'FOR THEM…The NHS, TV licences, Our schools, Child poverty, Grenfell, Crime victims, Homeless, Nurses VOTE LABOUR', 12 December 2019, *Daily Mirror*, courtesy of Mirrorpix/Reach Licensing; Table 5.1 contains information taken from www.abc.org.uk, used with permission; Tweets from Ben Bradshaw and Jeremy Corbyn used with permission; Extract in box 'Snapchat – capturing the youth vote' used with permission of Cast From Clay, https://castfromclay.co.uk/models-research/main-findings-social-media-demographics-uk-usa-2018/; Text within Figure 5.4 used with permission of the Conservative Party; Figure 5.5 is a PA Graphic, Source: NYU/Facebook; Tables 6.2 and 6.3 and 'Case study: Committee achievements in challenging government and influencing policy' contain information licensed under the Scottish Parliament Copyright Licence, www.parliament.scot/about/copyright; Pages 83–97 contain information licensed under the Scottish Parliament Copyright Licence; Extract from 'Offensive Behaviour at Football Act set to be abolished' by Tom Gordon, 15 May 2016, published in *The Herald*, used with permission; Paul Cairney (2013) 'How Can the Scottish Parliament Be Improved as a Legislature?' *Scottish Parliamentary Review*, 1, 1, 141–58; Extract from 'A Comprehensive Victory?' by Rebecca Montacute, 18 December 2019, used with permission of The Sutton Trust, www.suttontrust.com/news-opinion/all-news-opinion/a-comprehensive-victory/; Extract from 'Home Office chief Sir Philip Rutnam quits over Priti Patel "bullying"' by Aaron Walawalkar, 29 February 2020, *The Guardian*, © Guardian News & Media Ltd 2021; Content taken from www.england.nhs.uk/wp-content/uploads/2019/09/BM1917-NHS-recommendations-Government-Parliament-for-an-NHS-Bill.pdf contains public sector information licensed under the Open Government Licence v3.0; Content from www.cbi.org.uk/articles/the-latest-cbi-political-engagements-28-april/ used with permission of CBI; Content within Table 8.2 used with permission of The Joseph Rowntree Foundation; Content within the box '38 Degrees' used with permission of 38 Degrees; Content on allocation of marks copyright © Scottish Qualifications Authority; Table 9.1 copyright © Snap Surveys Limited 2021, reproduced with its permission, www.snapsurveys.com/blog/qualitative-vs-quantitative-research/.